Eddie Wolfie

Investment Manager

Founder of Lazy-Investing.com

Enthusiastic about stock market,

real estate, and cryptocurrency topics

Profiles:

Homepage: https://www.lazy-investing.com/

Medium: https://eddie-wolfie.medium.com/

LinkedIn: https://linkedin.com/in/eduardmeider/

Instagram: https://instagram.com/eddie.wolfie

CONTENT

DISCLAIMER

The information in this book is provided for education and informational purposes only, without any express or implied warranty of any kind. The information does not constitute financial advice, investment advice, trading advice or any other advice. The information in this book is general in nature and is not specific to you or anyone else. You should not make any decision, financial, investment, trading or otherwise based on any of the information presented in this book without undertaking independent due diligent and consultation with a professional broker or financial advisory.

INTRODUCTION

"It is well enough that people do not understand our banking and monetary system, for if they did, I believe there would be a revolution before tomorrow morning."

- Henry Ford -

We live in a centralized, unnecessarily complex world. Our existing financial system incentivizes behavior that is ultimately harmful. As a result, corruption, abuse of power, and inefficiency are all pervasive. State governments and monopolistic corporations establish more and more structures that make life difficult for us. They create opaque, slow bureaucracies that benefit themselves but prevent ordinary citizens from playing a role. The term moral hazard was coined to describe this problem. A moral hazard exists when economic agents behave irresponsibly or recklessly due to economic disincentives. Such behavior thereby triggers or amplifies a risk. The effects of moral hazards can be seen in the Henry Ford quote above. People would no longer tolerate the system if they had a better understanding of finance and economics.

The Western World believes that more control and supervision will solve these problems. Regulators, in their view, should introduce even stricter rules to combat the "evil machinations" of entrepreneurs. But this assessment ignores that most entrepreneurs and bankers only follow rules imposed by authorities. Moreover, history shows that centralized administrative economies are harmful to innovation, prosperity, and freedom. Excessive inter-vention in people's economic and social lives has dire consequences. The Roman Empire, the Soviet Union, and present-day Venezuela are just a few examples.

This book, however, is meant to convey the exact opposite. We need decentralized structures that are no longer controlled by individual institutions such as states. Such structures should be able to automatically regulate themselves through their system and network. The allocation of resources by inexperienced, unmotivated bureaucrats must be avoided. Decentralization creates the right incentives to allocate resources and finances more efficiently and fairly. It also leads to competition, which ensures that the best products and services prevail.

In 2009, Bitcoin emerged as the first decentralized cryptocurrency. It provided a new glimmer of hope for those pushing for decentralization. Bitcoin's set rules ensure its users a transparent experience. Without exception, anyone with an internet connection can access the cryptocurrency. Thus, no one is excluded from owning or trading it. Bitcoin is not governed by a single institution. Rather, it exists in a democratic system where transactions are validated in the blockchain. This ensures that the assets are not affected by harmful measures. It prevents devaluation of the cryptocurrency through, for example, the mass printing of money.

Other cryptocurrencies – even more technically mature than Bitcoin – have since been developed. Their business models show how previous financial services can be mapped in a decentralized manner. These models are collectively referred to as decentralized finance (DeFi).

In the first part of this book, you will learn about the theoretical principles behind DeFi. We will also discuss how it solves the problems of the classical financial system. The second part focuses on how you can currently use DeFi to generate passive income.

PART 1:

THEORETICAL BASICS OF DEFI

THE PROBLEMS OF THE CLASSICAL FINANCIAL SYSTEM

Cryptocurrencies and **decentralized applications (dApps)** are becoming increasingly popular. The traditional **centralized financial system (CeFi)** has shown increasing fragility, losing the trust of many. There are five main interconnected issues.

Business on a basis of trust

Many transactions – including contracts and financial transactions – are based on trust. They are conducted according to legal foundations, e.g., a signed contract in paper form. However, what matters is that people actually fulfill their promises in the end. Accidental and even deliberate breaches of contract are commonplace. Of course, such breaches have legal consequences, but lawsuits can be enormously expensive. Often, the resulting damages are not easy to prove. Furthermore, it is not uncommon for contracts to be circumvented through a backdoor.

When the Euro was introduced, governments stipulated that no direct sovereign financing could be provided to member countries. This is to prevent financially sensible nations from being liable for more reckless countries. In other words, those who do well are rewarded with low interest rates for government bonds. Those who manage money poorly are punished with higher interest rates. Ideally, they will then rethink their situation and create incentives for a better system.

In 2010, many southern European states in financial crisis found a way to undermine the law. These states are not financed in a direct way, but through an intermediary. This means that commercial banks buy the government bonds at inflated prices (equivalent to low interest rates). Usually, the commercial banks would not participate in this deal. However, the European Central Bank (ECB) guarantees them to immediately buy up the government bonds.

So, in economic terms, this is government financing, legally implemented through a backdoor. Thus, classic contracts and trust in parties are not sufficient to guarantee a secure transaction.

If greater sums are involved, contractual partners often involve a third party (e.g., a bank or a trustee). This third party acts as an intermediary. But this relationship is also based on a certain degree of trust. Trustees do not always behave neutrally and follow the interests of their primary clients.

Overregulation and misaligned incentives

Unlike central banks, commercial banks are strictly regulated by financial authorities. They must abide by the rules set for them. For example, banks cannot invest retail customers' money exclusively into high-risk financial products. Doing so would jeopardize the security of the money deposits. Some of these regulations are necessary. CeFi is based on trust, after all, and people need rules because their actions can be fallible. It becomes problematic, though, when bureaucrats decide when and how the rules apply. They then often exert more and more control, making the whole system far too complex and rigid.

The US government's influence was felt again through the Community Reinvestment Act (CRA). Mortgage banks were pressured to lend to creditworthy creditors, promoting real estate ownership, even in structurally weak regions. In this way, the government encouraged bad loans. It even had them bought up by state-owned banks, namely Fannie Mae and Freddie Mac.

These banks were securitized and guaranteed by the government's liability. This created an easy, artificial profit opportunity for lenders to package bundles of subprime loans. The bundles would then be sold to a government-backed buyer. The primary mandate was to "promote homeownership" rather than to follow sound lending standards. Under free market conditions, banks would not give "junk loans" to these people. However, this too-big-to-fail behavior created incentives for moral hazard. This was one of the causes of the 2007/2008 housing crisis in the US.

High fees for financial services

To operate in a trust-based CeFi system, commercial banks must be regulated by an external third party, such as a government agency. However, the financial sector is already too complex from over-regulation. Accordingly, commercial banks must spend excessive amounts of money on tax advisors and lawyers. This, in turn, further burdens customers in the end. For example, many banks cover their costs by charging fees just to manage checking accounts.

At other levels, intermediaries (trustees, notaries) must be involved, providing additional security for transactions. Of course, these services also incur fees.

Excessive money supply growth and inflation

As previously discussed, the goal of central banks is not only monetary stability. They are commonly influenced by politicians to serve their own purposes. To save financially weak European states, the base rate was lowered to 0%. On top of that, the money supply growth rate was massively expanded. This allowed states to borrow capital almost free of charge via bonds. However, such intervention in monetary policy results in the indirect expropriation of taxpayers.

Put simply, low interest rates and excessive increases in the money supply led to increased inflation (currency devaluation). The economy had more money available than before, but the quantity of goods remained the same. On the consumer level, we had just as much money as before, but we could afford less. It's possible that inflation was less noticeable according to the official consumer price index for daily good. However, the devaluation of money took place at the level of assets – e.g., real estate, whose prices multiplied from 2010 to 2020. At the same time, savers and risk-averse investors hardly receive any interest on their deposits. In the early 2000s, it was still common for risk-free investments to earn returns of around 3–4%. Since 2016, interest rates have partially dropped into negative territory. That meant we must give money to the state so that we could lend it to them.

Thus, we are witnessing governments brazenly expropriating their citizens while enriching themselves. Such systems show fragile characteristics that make survival much less sustainable. Negative incentives are created for states to fall deeper into debt without consolidating their fiscal spending. Such states expect to be bailed out by the central bank in the worst-case scenario.

Policymakers failing to rethink such systems could lead to hyperinflation in the future. That, in turn, could lead to the collapse of the traditional financial system.

Restricted access to financial services

More than two billion worldwide have no checking account or access to financial services. Developing countries often lack the necessary infrastructure, starting with a simple local bank branch. The usual bank customer also must undergo a personal identification process, meeting various requirements. For some people, this is impossible simply because they do not own passport documents.

As a result, these populations are dependent on cash and cannot store assets securely in checking accounts. They are also unable to invest in securities or take out loans.

Even in industrialized countries, financial services are not universally available. Others are only available for high fees. A simple example is foreign transfers of different currencies. They incur high transaction costs due to bureaucracy. In addition, regulations on investment products like private equity and venture capital can make them accessible only to certain investors. This is the case even though they are the ones generating high returns for professional investors.

THE DEFI ECOSYSTEM

DeFi refers to a financial system organized in a decentralized manner. Blockchains and smart contracts make up the technical foundation for this concept. They enable digital transactions to be carried out more transparently, efficiently, and securely without the involvement of central authorities. Below, you will find an excursus on both topics. Feel free to skip it if you are already familiar with those technologies. In addition, DeFi applications have three main characteristics, which are summarized in the chapter *The Three Pillars of DeFi*.

Excursus: Blockchain

A blockchain enables digital transactions between users to be processed without the data arriving at a central location like a bank. Instead, all transactions are recorded on a distributed ledger. There, they can be viewed transparently and publicly. More precisely, each participant can see how much money has been transferred between accounts. Conversely, they can see how much is in an account. The account holder is represented pseudonymously, with each account having a unique account number **(public key)**. It is not possible, however, to assign the public key to a living person in the analog world. The advantage of this system is that no central institution can delete the blockchain or log with the push of a button. Since the ledgers are stored on different computers **(full nodes)** around the world, this would not be technically possible.

Even if the internet fails worldwide, the protocol is stored offline. It can synchronize again as soon as the computers go online. You can see what such a ledger looks like at Blockchain.com.

The blockchain consists of an algorithm that automatically executes transactions when necessary contract conditions are met. No trust is needed from the contracting parties since the algorithm can be relied upon. This also eliminates the need for costly middlemen. Blockchain transactions are not limited to money transfers, though. They can also involve any information exchange, e.g., contracts, shares, or licenses. Thus, companies can provide smart contracts ensuring compliance in a transparent, neutral, and efficient manner.

Transactions on the blockchain generally incur smaller fees, which are urgently needed for decentralized settlements. They create an incentive for transactions to run smoothly without being manipulated. Democratic review processes take place for each transaction, considering several consensus processes. Basically, volunteer participants provide resources assisting in this **validation** process. In return for their services, these volunteers receive a portion of the transaction fees.

The best-known consensus method is **proof of work (PoW)**, which is used for Bitcoin. Several transactions are combined into a block and cryptographically encrypted. Then, so-called **miners** uncover this encryption by providing resources – the computing power. This is like guessing a code (**target hash**) with billions of attempts. Such a process requires a correspondingly large amount of power. Whoever contributes the most computing power has the greatest probability of solving this code.

The miner who decodes it first sends the information to the rest of the network. The information is validated by majority vote and appended to the blockchain.

However, a PoW blockchain can often suffer from scaling problems. More transactions being exercised on the blockchain result in greater power and transaction costs. To solve this problem, alternative blockchain methods have been developed based on the **Proof of Stake (PoS)** concept. These require significantly less overhead. The mechanism allows the number of coins – rather than computing power – to decide who validates the transactions. This procedure has proven itself, especially for cryptocurrencies in the DeFi area.

Excursus: Smart Contracts

Smart contracts are digital agreements in a blockchain that work according to a simplified scheme. If Condition X is fulfilled, then Y is triggered automatically. They are based on conventional legal contracts programmed by developers. The algorithm defines unambiguous conditions and actions. This assures all parties that contracts will be fulfilled without fraud or delay. All transactions are validated and logged on the blockchain, making them transparent and traceable. In an ideal situation, no trust is necessary for the contracting parties. Completely unrelated parties can complete transactions without needing an intermediary that incurs further fees. However, such automated contracts also require a greater sense of responsibility since blockchain transactions are generally non-reversible. A simple example of a smart contract transaction is the trading of different cryptocurrencies.

Peter wants to exchange two Bitcoin with Alex for 10 ether (**Ethereum**). For a successful transaction with a smart contract, both parties must fulfill three conditions:

1. Peter and Alex must have access to their **wallets**. This means their crypto accounts have private keys (personal passwords) and public keys (public account numbers).

2. Peter must own two Bitcoin in his wallet, and Alex must own 10 ether.

3. Peter and Alex must agree to the transaction exchanging two Bitcoin for 10 ether.

The smart contract will not be executed if one or both parties do not have enough cryptocurrencies. It also won't if they do not have account credentials or are not willing to make the exchange at all.

Smart Contract

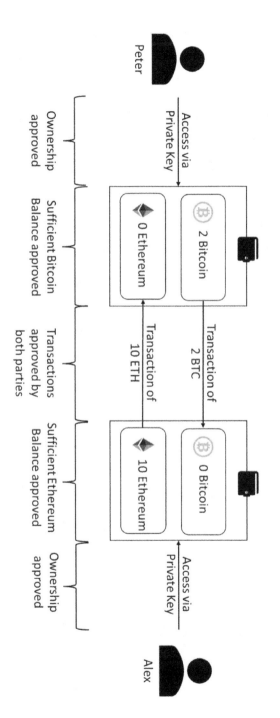

Imagine if we had processed a comparable transaction in the analog world. An intermediary (e.g., a trustee) would have to be involved. Otherwise, one of the two parties would have to make advance payments. The escrow solution would incur further fees. These are usually significantly higher than the transaction costs within a blockchain. In addition, the trustee solution slows down all transactions and fails to create a completely trust-free environment.

Without the middleman, the two could agree that Peter will pay in advance. He transfers two Bitcoin first. Alex then commits to transfer 10 ether to Peter within the next seven days. In daily life, Alex may forget the transaction, go bankrupt, die, or cheat. Until Peter gets his Bitcoins back, he must endure lots of stress. He'll possibly incur costs for lawyers until a solution is found after months or years. Such cases are commonplace in both private and business life. As such, they highlight the weaknesses of the legal system.

Trustee

Peter

Transfers 2 Bitcoin

Pays Fees

Receives 10 Ether

Trustee

Alex

Transfers 10 ETH

Pays Fees

Receives 2 Bitcoin

18

Smart contract use cases

The above is just one of the use cases where smart contracts could simplify our lives. The following are several other possible uses.

Supply chains: The blockchain documents when goods are received by participants in the supply chain. This triggers automatic actions – e.g., a purchase price payment – speeding up the process. It also creates transparency for each authorized person. For consumers, this can prove the authenticity of the product or its ecological value.

Real estate trading: Anyone purchasing property knows the effort involved in preparing all the documents for the notary. With a smart contract, this process can be completed without an intermediary. For example, an entry could be made automatically in a digital land register as soon as the contractual conditions are met.

Privacy: Information can be stored securely and digitally on the blockchain. Users can define ownership over items like patient records, sharing them only upon consent.

Insurances: Smart contracts are used to agree on the circumstances (e.g., a loss) for automatically paying insurance sums.

Licenses and copyright: For digital artworks, films, and music, ownership can be transparently represented and documented. So-called **NFTs (non-fungible tokens)** make it possible to trade, for example, digital trading cards. Ownership is transferred via the blockchain to prevent counterfeiting.

Policies: Policies are handled more transparently and efficiently via smart contracts. This includes party elections, distribution of subsidies, and tax payments, amongst others.

Smart contracts outlook

Smart contracts are in an early phase of their development cycle. With complex issues in the physical world, they reach their limits or require a supplementary human interface. These flaws, in turn, require trust. In addition, many traditional structures are not yet ready for digitization. As a result, such transactions are still carried out in paper form.

Furthermore, the quality of smart contracts will depend heavily on blockchain developers cooperating with lawyers. If digital contracts are programmed incorrectly, it will be difficult to correct or reverse transactions. Most users will not be able to cross-check the source code themselves. Thus, contracting parties will also have to continue placing trust in humans in the early stages. Reputable providers of smart contracts therefore rely on a strict security audit. Such a review guarantees that the contracts are free of errors.

In the financial services sector, digitization is already at an advanced stage. This means that many prerequisites for smart contracts in DeFi projects are already fulfilled today.

The three pillars of DeFi

Blockchains and smart contracts create the foundation for cryptocurrencies. These technologies, however, are not yet sufficient to enable a decentralized financial world. For this, the following three properties are complementarily necessary.

Permissionless: Being permissionless means that central authorities may not exclude users from participating in the system. This eliminates discrimination with respect to geographic location, origin, gender, or other attributes. The property is achieved by not subjecting users to registration or identity verification. They can create as many free accounts (wallets) as they wish, linking them to various financial applications. DeFi thereby enables everyone to participate in a global financial infrastructure on the internet.

Censorship resistant: Decentralized finance is intended to prevent the influence of censorship from politics and governments. This characteristic means decentralized platforms have no management or central administration carrying out official instructions. However, this does not mean that complete anarchy prevails. Most dApps are based on so-called **decentralized autonomous organizations (DAOs)**. These organizations enable their shareholders to vote democratically on the rules of the platform. Likewise, the applications are constantly being developed. However, they cannot make every decision on their own, relying on the consensus of their users.

Open source: Open source is software with publicly available source code. This allows external developers to verify that the programming is bug-free. They can also provide feedback on how to improve the application. Open source also makes it possible to copy the previous platform to program a better version. This creates diverse competition, which encourages users to choose the best service. Furthermore, open source creates transparency, eliminating the need for blind trust in the application. Everyone can see the functionality of the platform via the source code.

HOW DEFI SOLVES THE PROBLEMS OF THE CURRENT FINANCIAL SYSTEM

By applying blockchain technology and the pillars of DeFi, most financial system problems can be minimized. Others can be completely solved.

Business without a basis of trust

The use of smart contracts in legal transactions ensures that each party fulfills its expectations. This means that trusting the reliability of the other party is no longer a prerequisite. The programmed algorithm leaves nothing to do but execute the contract. Accordingly, there is no need for intermediaries (i.e., lawyers and trustees) to monitor the process.

Applying this at the political level, e.g., for a currency, results in greater stability and planning security. Politicians could no longer interpret existing laws at their own discretion. Instead, they would have to abide by the agreements. Deviation from the EU Treaty, such as indirect state financing, would have been impossible without dissolving and renegotiating the treaty. Smart contracts help maintain room to maneuver when bailing out indebted states. In this case, states receive a cash injection that is tied to strict conditions and collateral. This could be such that sovereigns deposit existing assets (e.g., gold reserves, land, etc.) as collateral.

Those assets are automatically transferred to the creditor if milestones like timely repayment are not met.

Overall, smart contracts prove that contracting parties take the agreements seriously and follow them. Thus, contracts can be created between all people and institutions, even if they are completely unknown.

Meaningful incentives

One of the purposes of regulation is to minimize human error such as in the performance of contracts. However, smart contracts do not require trust in the contracting parties. Digital contracts on the blockchain consequently require little to no regulation by central institutions. This is because they are executed automatically by a tamper-proof algorithm and controlled by the network.

DeFi services are also organized in a decentralized manner and can be accessed globally. This broadly distributed network makes regulation much more difficult. In some cases, it becomes impossible.

In the CeFi system, our money is held in a bank account that is subject to national laws. The state deciding to intervene in an extreme way can devalue our property by law without the use of force. An example of this would include a currency reform. However, let's say we own cryptocurrencies in a decentralized wallet. No state institution (at least without the threat of force) has the possibility to get hold of our assets. Nor will they be able to decide that the assets are no longer worth anything.

Finally, decentralization ensures the application of fair market mechanisms. Bureaucrats can no longer make arbitrary decisions, while market participants democratically regulate themselves.

A decentralized application that does not function effectively must face competitive pressure. It will either be improved or replaced by a better program from the competition. This logic creates the right incentives to avoid corruption and errors.

It's easy to think of this in terms of currency. State governments often force their citizens to use only the national currency as a medium of exchange. The governments can then exercise control over the economy and society. This concept becomes problematic in countries with unstable financial systems. If these suffer from higher inflation rates, their cash is devalued almost daily. As a result, citizens often secretly resort to more stable foreign currencies. In doing so, they build up a black market where goods can only be paid for with foreign currency. This problem would not even exist in a decentralized system. Users could legally choose a currency themselves. Through freedom of choice, the best currency would automatically prevail. That currency would then be accepted by most people as a means of payment. Weak, corrupt currency systems would be forgotten – deservedly so.

Low fees

Decentralized finance dispenses with intermediaries and requires fewer regulations. There is less bureaucracy from the outset. State borders can disappear thanks to foreign currencies, often causing higher costs for financial transactions.

A functioning DeFi network does not require an institution such as a bank setting fees for transactions. However, it is not possible to completely dispense all costs in DeFi systems. There are always fees that must be paid to the network for the execution of smart contracts to validate blockchain transactions.

Admittedly, some of these fees were higher than in the CeFi sector in 2021. Frequently used blockchain networks such as Ethereum recorded such high demand that transaction costs skyrocketed. Technically, there was a lack of a scaling solution. This will be solved with the new update – **Ethereum 2.0**. Incidentally, it can be observed that the DeFi ecosystem can quickly solve such problems itself. For this purpose, smart contract platforms were launched to execute decentralized services significantly faster and cheaper. These include **Polygon**, **Fantom**, and **Avalanche**.

Fair asset development

Decentralized finance operates autonomously and without the intervention of a central bank. No monetary policy is exercised according to political criteria. All measures are determined by the consensus of the users.

This includes the agreed-upon money supply growth, which is decided according to smart contract algorithm. This logic could be applied to an economic system to avoid currency inflation. For example, a smart contract could regulate the money supply's automatic growth proportional to economic growth. In parallel, investors would have access to Bitcoin with a fixed maximum quantity. This offers an additional deflationary real asset that guarantees the stability of their assets.

By applying such a market mechanism, government institutions would ideally borrow money through the economic system rather than from the central bank. This would create fair interest rate conditions according to supply and demand for debtors and creditors. It would also avoid indirect expropriation through inflation.

Free accessibility

DeFi applications do not require user verification. Anyone of any nationality or origin can access the services. An internet-enabled device, such as a smartphone, is all that is needed to create a wallet. Cryptocurrencies can then be stored and transferred to other wallets. Users can trade, earn interest on their savings, or even take out loans. This would be a major milestone, especially for people in developing countries without access to financial services.

PART 2:

PRACTICAL APPLICATION OF DEFI

The considerations so far, while theoretical, show the disruptive possibilities of decentralized finance. Let's take a closer look at the topic, examining what is already possible in practice.

DEFI:
WHAT IS ALREADY POSSIBLE TODAY?

DeFi experienced high growth in 2020 and 2021, already attracting over $100 billion in investor funds. This key metric is referred to as **total value locked (TVL)**. It corresponds to the assets, converted into U.S. dollars, that have been invested as cryptocurrencies in DeFi applications.

Despite its high volume, DeFi is still in an early stage. Many of our economy's non-digitized processes cannot yet be mapped and automated in a blockchain. In addition, most securities traded in the financial market are regulated by government agencies. This means their trading is only available to licensed partners. DeFi apps, in turn, do not have direct access to these products. If the traditional system prevails, DeFi users must make compromises. In a **decentralized exchange**, for example, it is only possible to exchange cryptocurrencies for each other. However, if you want to convert your coins into **fiat money** – e.g., U.S. dollars – you still rely on **central exchanges**.

The processes leading to the use of decentralized applications can be cumbersome for beginners. It is advisable not to start blindly. You should familiarize yourself with the world of cryptocurrencies, trying it out with small amounts first. For this purpose, various tutorials have been published on YouTube to help you along the way. Furthermore, so-called **CeDeFi** platforms offer a compromise, applying various DeFi solutions via a central interface. Regulated companies like Cake DeFi* allow you to directly transfer fiat money to an online wallet. You can then exchange it against cryptocurrencies. Thus, you'll be able to work without further detours from decentralized applications.

The use cases of decentralized apps are very diverse. Below, you will find a categorization of the areas covered by DeFi. Then, you will learn how using them practically can generate passive income.

*Using the following invitation link for Cake DeFi, you will receive a $30 bonus paid in cryptocurrency DFI when you make an investment of at least $50: cakedefi.com/?ref=074201

DECENTRALIZED VALUE

On the Internet of Value, it is possible to store and transfer financial value digitally. Decentralized value goes one step further, enabling the decentralized storage of assets. Thus, they are not documented on a central platform. Rather, they are logged on a blockchain – i.e., in globally distributed protocols. No one can erase this asset due to the backup copy on the network.

However, state institutions cannot implement a devaluation or expropriation of decentralized assets. This is especially true since the blockchain is not limited by national borders. In financial crises like hyperinflation, even analogous tangible assets such as real estate cannot provide sufficient protection. In the last century, wealthy people have been expropriated (including house searches). At the least, they are burdened with wealth taxes. Such scenarios are less likely for cryptocurrencies, as proving their ownership is more complex. The authorities make it easy for themselves. They will often only charge assets that can be easily proven. This includes real estate, shares, and bank accounts. Cryptocurrencies as a decentralized store of value have clear advantages in such worst-case scenarios.

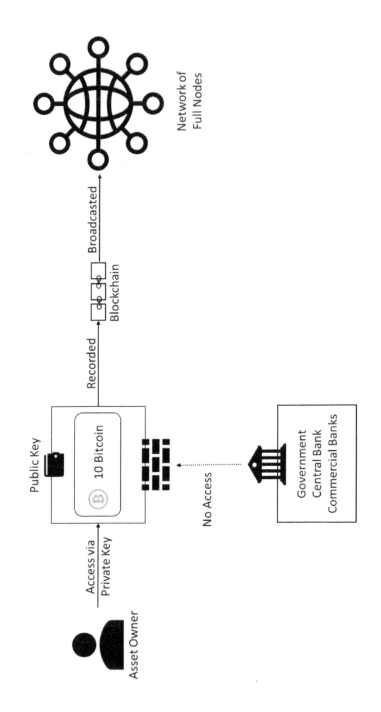

Decentralized Value

Network of
Full Nodes

Broadcasted

Blockchain

Recorded

Public Key

10 Bitcoin

No Access

Government
Central Bank
Commercial Banks

Access via
Private Key

Asset Owner

Centralized Value

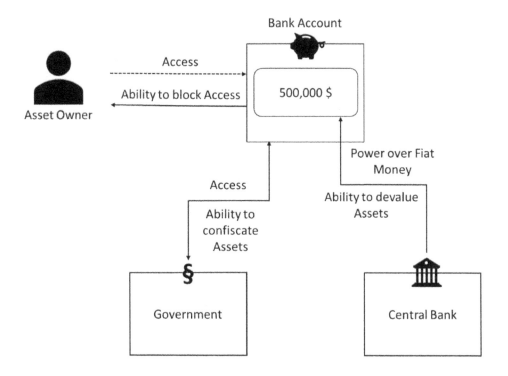

A common criticism of digital assets is that they are not tangible. They exist only in a virtual world, unable to be touched in a physical way. Many investors believe that, with gold or real estate, you own something real. To them, that's the only way actual value exists. However, this view is outdated. According to this logic, fiat currencies would not represent value either. After all, they are just printed paper with no added value. Furthermore, businesses commonly assign a balance sheet value to so-called intangible assets. For example, user rights and licenses offer added value to market participants. Those participants are thus prepared to pay a price.

Digital Gold

The simplest example of a decentralized asset is Bitcoin – the oldest, most established cryptocurrency. The crypto community refers to it as digital gold due to its similar characteristics. The coin enjoys a high level of trust. It has a certain stability in value, at least in the long term. Technically, Bitcoin already fulfills the requirements of a rare asset today. New coins can only be mined with considerable effort. Their total number is limited. The result is its deflationary character. In theory, this leads to a steady increase in value compared to inflationary fiat currencies. In addition, Bitcoin has the advantage over precious metals. Its digital storage and transfer are much more efficient.

Non-Fungible Tokens

Non-fungible tokens (NFTs) are another option for the decentralized storage of assets. They are digital objects that cannot be exchanged or copied. This contrasts with currencies, which are exchangeable without loss of value. A Bitcoin is always worth as much as another Bitcoin. An NFT is never exactly equal to the value of another NFT. In other words, each token is unique. A virtual artwork is a simple example. It can be uniquely assigned to its owner on the blockchain. Thus, both digital currencies (fungible tokens) and user rights can be stored and exchanged. Imagine a digitally drawn Mona Lisa with enormous collector value due to its authenticity. If someone takes a screenshot, its originality could not be identified on the blockchain. The copy would consequently be worth nothing.

NFTs such as the well-known Crypto Punks and Crypto Kitties can be purchased at Opensea.io.

Stablecoins

Stablecoins are cryptocurrencies that replicate the value of a currency or asset as closely as possible. The best-known stablecoins are linked to the value of the U.S. dollar. These include **USD Coin (USDC)**, **USD Tether (USDT)**, and **DAI**. One unit of such tokens is exactly equal in value to one U.S. dollar. Other stablecoins replicate the values of cryptocurrencies so they can be traded on different blockchains. For this purpose, the corresponding counterparts **Wrapped Bitcoin (WBTC)** and **Wrapped Ethereum (WETH)** were developed for Bitcoin and Ethereum. Most recently, stablecoins have even tracked the value of commodities and precious metals. The most notable is **PAX Gold**. Its token is equivalent to the value of an ounce of gold.

Reliable stablecoin providers optimally deposit 100% of the currency to be replicated with a trustee. With the centrally organized USDC token, the same number of coins in circulation is always deposited with a trustee. They are deposited in the form of real U.S. dollars. The higher the demand for the USDC token, the more units of U.S. dollars are deposited with the trustee, and vice versa. When in doubt, investors can always exchange USDC tokens 1:1 for real U.S. dollars.

Stablecoin (CeFi)

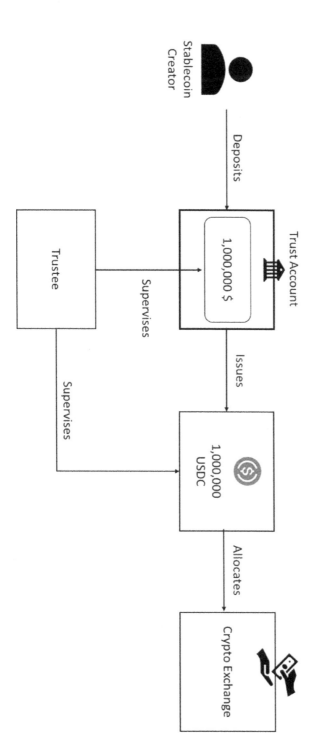

The decentralized provider **MakerDAO**, in turn, issues DAI tokens (one DAI = one U.S. dollar). This is accomplished by depositing other cryptocurrencies as collateral. This collateral must always be higher in dollar value than the circulating DAI tokens. For example, in the chart below, twice as many Bitcoins were deposited as collateral as DAIs were created in value (LTV = 0.50; see also later subsection *Decentralized Lending*). The created stablecoins are a kind of loan on which the issuer has to pay regular interest. He can repay this loan at any time. Doing so would reduce the number of DAI tokens in circulation. In this case, the tokens are destroyed again. This principle allows any user to issue any number of stablecoins. The user is then able to trade them freely in the market. This is possible as long as sufficient collateral is deposited and interest is paid.

Stablecoins combine the worlds of CeFi and DeFi. They enable traditional financial products like fiat currencies to be traded on the blockchain. At the same time, they create access to stable fiat currencies for every user worldwide. In some cases, they are even completely decentralized, without prior registration on a platform. Stablecoins also allow investors to exchange their more volatile cryptocurrencies quickly and cheaply. In return, they get less volatile tokens and park them there.

Stablecoin (DeFi)

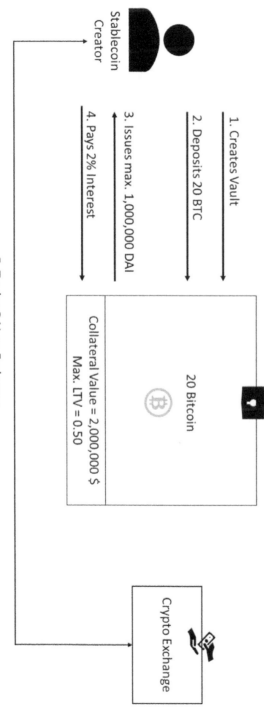

Stablecoin
Creator

1. Creates Vault

2. Deposits 20 BTC

3. Issues max. 1,000,000 DAI

4. Pays 2% Interest

20 Bitcoin

Collateral Value = 2,000,000 $
Max. LTV = 0.50

5. Trades DAI on Exchange

Crypto Exchange

DECENTRALIZED TRANSFER

Decentralized transfers mostly occur in the form of **decentralized exchange** platforms (**DEXs**). They allow users to swap cryptocurrencies and other tokenized assets without the intervention of central authorities.

Classical exchanges work according to the principle of an order book. Each user enters his desired conditions for a buy or sell order. These conditions include the exchange rate (e.g., how much Bitcoin one would like to receive per U.S. dollar) andthe quantity (e.g., how much Bitcoin one would like to receive in total). These orders are first collected in the order book. Then, they trigger a transaction as soon as the buy and sell rates meet. Traditional exchanges are usually highly regulated. Therefore, they must meet various requirements, including the verification of their customers. This is done with the **know your customer** (**KYC**) guidelines. Decentralized exchanges, on the other hand, are based on smart contracts on the blockchain. This means they do not require a centrally regulated platform. A web or smartphone application creates an interface enabling users to access smart contracts. All they do is connect their wallets with the platform without verifying their identity.

Automated market making

The interesting question now is how trading works without order books or central intermediaries.
For this, most DEXs use an **automated market maker** (**AMM**). In an AMM, two counterparts interact via a **liquidity pool**.

Trader: Traders are those who want to swap currency pairs. For example, when they trade Bitcoin for USDC, they put Bitcoin into the pool. Then, they receive USDC back from the pool. In addition, traders pay a small fee for executing the order. On the most popular DEX, UniSwap, this fee is 0.3% of the exchange volume.

Liquidity provider: Liquidity providers (**LPs**) put currency pairs into a liquidity pool at a ratio of 1:1. An example would be 50% Bitcoin and 50% USDC. Then, traders can exchange the corresponding currencies as described above. For providing the liquidity, the LPs receive a share of the traders' order fees. This process is explained in more detail in the later chapter on **liquidity mining**.

Decentralized Exchange

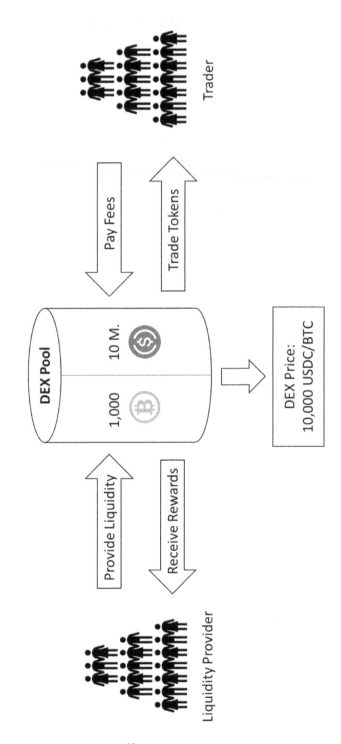

Pricing

The currency pair is priced according to the ratio of the two currencies in the liquidity pool.

Example: There are currently 1,000 Bitcoin and 10,000,000 USDC in the currency pair's total liquidity pool. Thus, traders can either exchange 1 Bitcoin for 10,000 USDC or 10,000 USDC for 1 Bitcoin. What if the ratio in the liquidity pool changes? Let's say only 500 Bitcoin are available and 10,000,000 USDC continue to be available. The price will then be 20,000 USDC/BTC analogously.

Automated market making enables prices in line with the market without intermediaries and regulation. For the principle to work effectively, the decentralized exchange must already have a high volume of users and a high liquidity to form prices as close to reality as possible.

Price arbitrage

The AMM reaches its limits when only smaller liquidity pools are formed. Larger trading volumes can cause a significant price drop, though usually in the short-term. This is quickly offset by arbitrageurs exploiting the price deviation between decentralized and centralized exchanges.

Let's assume liquidity providers invest the equivalent of $2,000,000. Thereby, they provide liquidity for the ETH and USDC currency pair. Accordingly, a total of 200 ETH and 1,000,000 USDC are deposited. Through this ratio, they determine an exchange rate of 1 ETH = 5,000 USDC. This is also the market price on other crypto exchanges.

DEX Price Arbitrage

State 1:

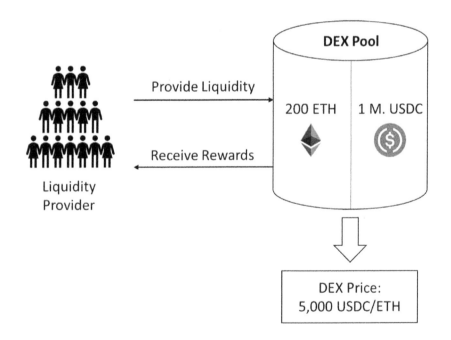

A trader now wants to exchange 50 ETH for 200,000 USDC. Simply put, 50 ETH flow into the liquidity pool and 200,000 USDC are withdrawn. The new ratio is 250 ETH to 800,000 USDC, for a new purchase price of 1 ETH = 3,200 USDC. As a result, the liquidity providers have less ETH and more USDC in their possession. Both, however, still have the same total value of $2 million.

DEX Price Arbitrage

State 2:

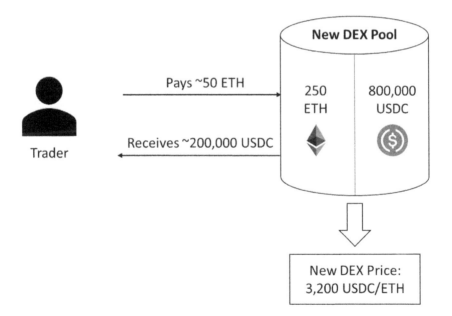

The new exchange rate of 1 ETH = 3,200 USDC is only available on this DEX. A rate of 1 ETH = 5,000 USDC continues, however, to be paid on other exchanges. This imbalance attracts arbitrageurs. They would then exchange as much ETH for USDC until the original exchange ratio on the DEX moves back to 1 ETH = 5,000 USDC. They would have to add about 175,680 USDC to the pool, withdrawing about 55 ETH. (The rough calculation serves for understanding this process. An approximation function is applied so the arbitrageur doesn't receive a rate of 3,200 USDC/ETH for the full amount.)

DEX Price Arbitrage

State 3:

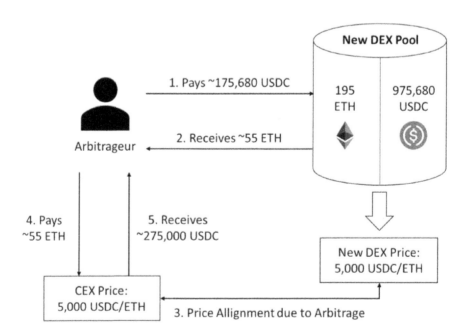

The previously more favorable price for ETH on DEX allows the arbitrageurs, in turn, to sell ETH at a profit. They conduct this sale on another exchange where the ETH to USDC exchange ratio is higher.

The above example is, of course, an extreme case. On most decentralized exchanges, liquidity is high enough that such price collapses rarely occur. The instance illustrates how liquidity providers, traders, and arbitrageurs bring the AMM system into equilibrium. More information on arbitrage will follow in a later chapter.

Slippage:

With smaller liquidity pools, it is possible for the ratio of the currency pairs to experience short-term change. Consequently, the price will change significantly. In the case of higher trading volumes, this can trigger a so-called **slippage**. For example, you expect to trade ether for USDC at a rate of 4,000 USDC/ETH. However, by the moment of execution, the rate changes to 3,950 USDC/ETH. That corresponds to a slippage of 1.25%. You are no longer willing to make the exchange at this rate, but you cannot reverse it. To solve this problem, decentralized exchanges allow you to adjust a **slippage tolerance** beforehand. If the setting is too low, though, your transaction may not be executed immediately.

Advantages of decentralized exchanges

No regulation: Decentralized exchanges are not accountable to any authority, unlike centralized exchanges. They cannot be shut down or restricted by any central institution. Therefore, cryptocurrencies can often temporarily become unable to be traded or transferred on centralized exchanges. Likewise, decentralized exchanges are not subject to KYC regulations. They require neither registration nor legitimation of their users. Anyone in the world thus has immediate access to the exchange.

Higher selection: On decentralized exchanges, the listing of new tokens is much less bureaucratic. Theoretically, anyone can offer new cryptocurrencies for exchange by applying liquidity mining. This process is significantly more time-consuming and costly for centralized exchanges until approval is granted. Decentralized exchanges usually offer significantly more coins from which to choose.

Security: Established DEXs are secure and respectable because their code is visible to all users. Possible programming errors in the blockchain can be detected by the larger community. For many users, it is also crucial that the credit is not stored on the exchange but on their own wallet anonymously. In extreme cases, your assets would be more secure. Such scenarios include expropriations ordered by the authorities or hacker attacks.

Low fees: Decentralized exchanges are leanly organized and, consequently, incur fewer costs. Nevertheless, it is not always possible to assume whether they are more favorable for the trader than central exchanges. Based on order costs, decentralized exchanges are usually cheaper than centralized exchanges (except Binance). However, on DEXs, there are additional transaction costs for the blockchain. These can be high or low depending on trading volume and choice of network. For this purpose, it is recommended you compare the expected fees on different platforms.

Provider of decentralized exchanges

The best-known providers of decentralized exchanges include:

- UniSwap
- Curve Finance
- PancakeSwap
- SushiSwap

Particularly noteworthy is UniSwap's DEX. The platform enables the trading of over 2,000 different currency pairs. It reaches a TVL of currently $10.5 billion. Approximately $3 billion in cryptocurrencies are traded daily. The platform was created in 2018 and has continued to improve in the following years. Its third version (UniSwap V3) was already launched in 2021. For each trade, UniSwap charges a fee of 0.3%. In addition, transaction costs are charged for the blockchain.

In the appendix, you will find instructions on decentralized exchanges using UniSwap as an example.

DECENTRALIZED LENDING

With decentralized lending, creditors and debtors can extend credit without banks or other intermediaries. Comparable to a decentralized stock exchange, lenders provide liquidity for a pool. In turn, they receive an interest rate as compensation. Similarly, borrowers can draw on this liquidity pool, with an interest rate as their fee.

Interest Rate

The interest rate is usually variable. It is calculated with a formula according to supply and demand. Simply put, if more loans are demanded, borrowers must pay correspondingly higher interest rates. Sometimes, there is a lot of liquidity in the pool, which is less in demand. As a result, interest rates fall. However, some providers also offer fixed interest rates over longer periods.

Duration

The platforms also offer different solutions regarding run-times. With centralized lending service providers, fixed contract terms (e.g., six months) are common. Decentralized applications have unlimited terms if the loan – including interest – does not exceed the **collateral** limit.

Collateral

As usual, loans cannot simply be granted without collateral. In CeFi, the simplest example is the deposit of property as collateral (mortgage loan). In this case, the bank leaves an entry of its right to the property in the land register. Thus, it can auction it off in the event of insolvency.

In DeFi, this process is organized in a more streamlined manner. It can be illustrated using the provider **Aave** in the following figure.

On Aave, you can deposit a cryptocurrency as collateral. This creates a so-called **vault**, a kind of safe into which you transfer, for example, Bitcoin. The smart contract then allows you to borrow another cryptocurrency, for instance, the DAI token.

Due to the volatile crypto market, strict conditions often apply when depositing collateral. In technical jargon, this is referred to as the **loan-to-value (LTV) ratio**. The LTV measures the ratio of the loan amount to the collateral. Alternatively, some dApps use the term **collateralization ratio**, which conversely measures the ratio of the collateral to the loan amount.

In most cases, the collateral deposited in the vault must be significantly higher in value than the loan. Here, we speak of an over-collateralization. This rule prevents the value of the collateral from falling below the loan amount from price fluctuations. Such a drop in value may prevent the creditor from being paid. In the example above, say you deposit $10,000 in Bitcoin. Then, you are allowed to borrow $5,000 in DAI with it. This corresponds to an LTV of 0.50 (or a collaterization ratio of 200%).

Decentralized Lending

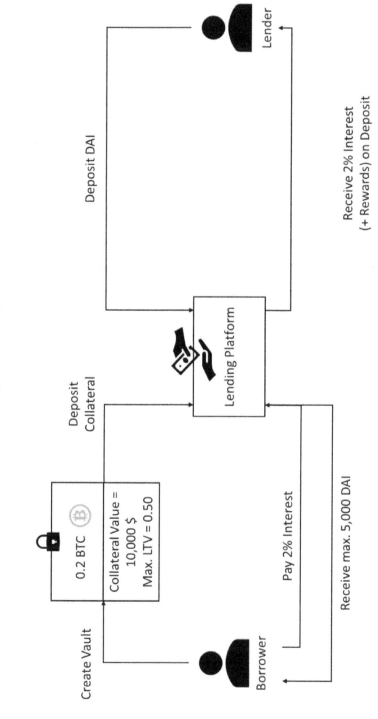

You will also get better interest rates as a borrower if you put down even more collateral. This is the case on some lending platforms, like **DeFiChain**. With an LTV of 0.50, the interest rate is 2% p.a. With an LTV of 0.10, the interest rate drops to 0.5%.

Technically, it would also be possible in the future to deposit tokenized shares, real estate, and other assets as collateral.

Insolvency

Insolvency of the debtor occurs when the value of the collateral falls below the collateral limit. A tolerance value (**liquidation threshold**) is usually defined for this. If it is exceeded, it triggers the liquidation of the collateral. This means the borrower's collateral is automatically sold to repay the loan, including interest. The difference that remains is returned to the borrower, minus a fee (**liquidation penalty**). To prevent such a scenario, the borrower must increase his collateral early on. Additionally, they could prevent it by repaying a partial amount of the loan.

For example, we borrow 30,000 DAI for one month and deposit 1 Bitcoin as collateral. At a rate of 60,000 DAI/BTC, this corresponds to a coverage of 200% (LTV = 0.50). Let's assume the liquidation threshold is at 130%. After one week, the Bitcoin drops to 40,000 USDC/BTC, leaving the loan only 133% covered. So, the loan is at risk and about to be liquidated. The collateral must therefore be increased. That is, more Bitcoin must be deposited in the vault. Alternatively, DAI must be paid back. On the other hand, Bitcoin may increase in value against DAI (e.g., to 80,000 DAI/BTC).

This creates the possibility to borrow more DAI [here: maximum 80,000 USDC/200% = 40,000 DAI].

Use Case

Now, the question arises why one would want to lend cryptocurrencies at all. Why even deposit collateral in the form of other cryptocurrencies for this purpose? One could simply exchange the cryptocurrencies with each other, saving interest. However, many investors do not want to sell their existing cryptocurrencies. They would prefer to offer them as collateral. This is because, on the one hand, the cryptocurrency held could increase in value. On the other hand, the direct exchange of two cryptocurrencies is equivalent to a sale of the asset. The exchange would trigger taxes on the previous price increase.

Currently, the loans are mostly used for **leverage investments** and **short positions**. Investors take out additional credit to invest in cryptocurrencies with greater leverage. Imagine, for example, that you pay only 2% interest but make 10% return. Then, it's worth borrowing even more to increase your profit.

We would like to take a short position on the US dollar. This means we speculate that Bitcoin will rise in value against the stablecoin USDC. As in the example above, 1 Bitcoin currently corresponds to the value of 60,000 USDC. First, we deposit 1 Bitcoin as collateral, receiving a loan of 30,000 USDC. This loan accrues 10% interest. At the year's end, we must pay back 33,000 USDC (including 3,000 USDC interest).

We immediately exchange the 30,000 USDC from the loan into Bitcoin via an exchange. This gives us 0.5 BTC for it. After one year, it turns out that our forecast was correct. Bitcoin has risen from 60,000 USDC/BTC to 100,000 USDC/BTC in the meantime.

To close the short position, we must pay back our debt in USDC. We exchange Bitcoins for USDC on the exchange until reaching 33,000 USDC. With the exchange rate above, that's 33,000 USDC divided by 100,000 USDC/BTC. This gives us 0.33 BTC. After we have settled the loan, we receive our collateral in the amount of 1 Bitcoin.

Ultimately, we only had to pay back 0.33 BTC of the 0.5 BTC we borrowed. This leaves us holding 0.17 more Bitcoin than we did a year earlier. At the same time, the value of Bitcoin has grown. Thus, our assets have increased from the original $60,000 to $117,000.

It's true that most loans are still used for speculative purposes. However, they are also eligible for consumption or short-term payment of bills in everyday life.

Advantages of decentralized lending

Low credit default risk: Lending technically always has a default risk if the borrower cannot repay the amount. The big advantage in the DeFi ecosystem is that almost all loans are over-collateralized. Borrowers must always deposit more assets as collateral than the equivalent value they can lend in the loan. This design makes a default very unlikely. Theoretically, it could only occur under one condition. When the value of the collateral falls massively so quickly that timely liquidation is no longer possible.

Let's use the example from the *Insolvency* section above. Bitcoin must fall by more than 35% within seconds for this to occur.

Accessibility: Through decentralized credit financing, anyone with internet access can take out a loan. They no longer need to involve a bank. This creates significant advantages in developing countries lacking financial infrastructure. It also benefits small- and medium-sized enterprises in industrialized countries. Previously, such businesses had to struggle with bureaucracy and high costs when raising debt.

Fair and transparent conditions: The terms for decentralized loans are openly visible, with fair principles for all parties. This is due to the open-source platform, free-market mechanisms, and absence of bank policies.

For the smart contract, your background, profession, and anything else is completely irrelevant. You simply must provide sufficiently high collaterals.

Source of income for savers: Decentralized lending provides a lucrative source of income for savers. This is especially true given the current artificial zero interest rate for fiat currencies. Excess assets can be deposited into the liquidity pool to generate interest rates. Such rates are usually in the higher single digits per year.

TOKENIZATION

Tokenization is the denomination of an asset into a digital security on the blockchain. All assets whose rights can be represented digitally are eligible for tokenization. This includes classic investment products such as shares, real estate, corporate bonds, ETFs, and precious metals. It also involves alternative tangible assets such as art, classic cars, and spirits.

For example, a property could be tokenized so that it no longer belongs 100% to one owner. Instead, it would be distributed among several investors. More precisely, these are ownership rights that can be purchased by investors at certain prices. Later, they can be traded on an exchange. If the property generates income, the proceeds flow proportionately back to its owners.

In tokenization, there are key differences between CeFi's regulated securities (**security tokens**) and DeFi's unregulated decentralized assets (**dTokens**).

Tokenization CeFi

Traditionally, tokenization in CeFi works according to the following principle. First, the issuer deposits proof of ownership of a target object with a trustee. Such objects can include a company, real estate, or another asset. Next, a new investment company is founded. In technical jargon, this is called a **special purpose vehicle (SPV)**. This participates in the target property in the form of equity, mezzanine capital, or loans. Thus, it is entitled to its proceeds. The SPV company, in turn, issues tokenized bonds to its investors. These bonds are stored in their wallets. Investors can usually purchase token shares with low investment volumes, e.g., starting at $500. The target object generates revenues that are verifiable via, for example, annual financial statements. In this case, the smart contract ensures proceeds are distributed to the token investors.

Tokenizations are currently monitored by national financial supervisions. They are subject to strict rules. Investors must also have their identities verified. These measures create legal certainty between the digital and analog worlds.

Tokenization (CeFi)

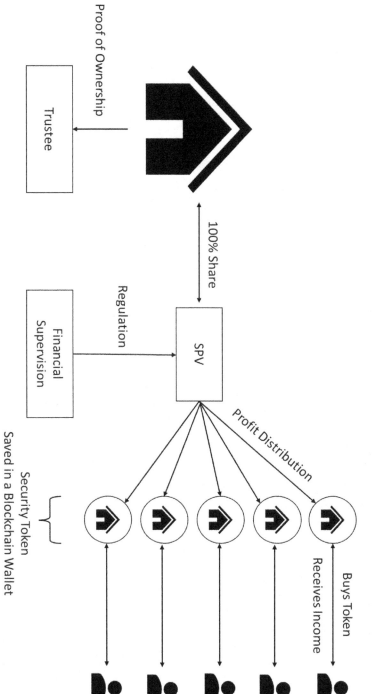

Proof of Ownership

Trustee

100% Share

Regulation

Financial Supervision

SPV

Profit Distribution

Security Token Saved in a Blockchain Wallet

Receives Income

Buys Token

Tokenization DeFi

In the DeFi world, tokenizations are not regulated. All users can mint tokens. Simply, this is a lending of the asset comparable to decentralized lending in principle. First, cryptocurrencies are deposited as collateral in a vault. Then, decentralized tokens can be issued at a predefined share of the collateral.

As an example, let's say we want to issue a token of a Tesla stock. It is currently traded on central exchanges at a price of $1,000. For this, we create a vault and deposit $2,000 worth of Bitcoin as collateral. For 50% of the value in the vault, we are allowed to mint decentralized assets. In this case, this value is equivalent to $1,000 or one Tesla share. The tokenized Tesla share can then be traded on decentralized exchanges. It can also be deposited for liquidity mining (see later chapter).

The blockchain receives information on the worth of the decentralized asset (the Tesla share). It receives the market worth at any time via a so-called **Oracle**. What if the dToken's value rises while the cryptocurrency deposited in the vault stagnates? The issuer must increase the collateral. If he doesn't, he risks the liquidation of his collateral when the threshold is exceeded.

Tokenization (DeFi)

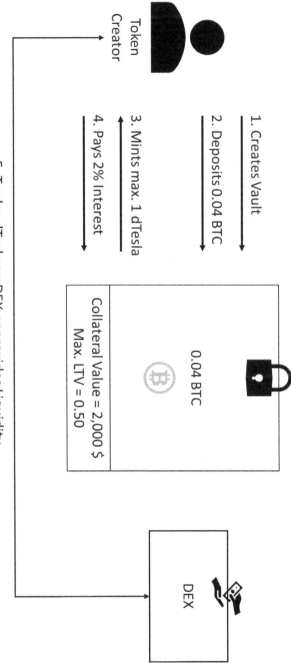

Token Creator

1. Creates Vault

2. Deposits 0.04 BTC

3. Mints max. 1 dTesla

4. Pays 2% Interest

5. Trades dTesla on DEX or provides Liquidity

0.04 BTC

Collateral Value = 2,000 $
Max. LTV = 0.50

DEX

Advantages of tokenization

Suppose a small- or medium-sized company in the CeFi world wants to finance itself. It usually incurs high costs for regulatory structuring. This includes it going public or launching a fund or bond. In contrast, tokenization enables digital and more streamlined issuance of financial products. It saves companies from incurring many fees.

The use of smart contracts is also a major plus from an investor's point of view. The rights and obligations of the contracting parties are clearly defined and executed automatically. Ownership is not deposited on a central server. Instead, it is organized via the blockchain. There is reduced risk of the issuer delaying profit distributions or withholding them without permission. Lastly, tokenization has the advantage because digital securities are tradable at low unit costs. This gives smaller investors access to new opportunities.

In DeFi, tokenization helps synthetically replicate already issued financial products. Due to the lack of regulation, anyone can invest in these decentralized assets with micro amounts. They can profit from the performance of stocks and ETFs, even if they have no bank account access.

Tokenization outlook

Tokenization has huge potential but is still at an early stage of development. Many processes cannot yet be represented digitally on a blockchain. Thus, interfaces in the analog world are still needed.

This problem can be easily illustrated with the example of a tokenized property. The property generates rental income. Individual tenants transfer it to a traditional bank account – not to a blockchain wallet. Furthermore, the building may be unexpectedly damaged, requiring repairs. In these cases, token holders rely on the landlord. The landlord must properly document all actions on the blockchain. This ensures that proceeds are correctly distributed to investors. However, this brings us back to the original problem of CeFi. The system requires trust in the contracting parties. Apart from that, the land register is also not yet mapped on a blockchain. Legally speaking, the property can only change its owner in the analog world.

If digitization advances in the future, tokenization could be further decentralized. Technically, it should be possible to represent companies' accounting and the land register for real estate in a blockchain. This opens up various new possibilities for making assets digitally tradable. One's own valuables (e.g., expensive watches, artwork, cars) could be represented as tokens. They could be deposited as collateral to take out a loan on a lending platform. Theoretically, it would also be possible to tokenize future salary to obtain immediate liquidity. In this case, the token owner receives a right to a share of the issuer's future income.

Tokenization provider

The pioneer in decentralized tokenization is Mirror Finance. The app allows existing shares or ETFs to be issued and traded as dTokens. For example, you can participate in the performance of Tesla, Apple, or MSCI World. You could also generate passive income through liquidity mining (covered in upcoming chapters). In the appendix, you will find instructions on decentralized tokenization using Mirror Finance.

If you are looking for a less complicated way to trade tokenized assets, you should also try the platform Cake DeFi*. They offer to deposit fiat money directly and allow you to trade it for dTokens on the DeFiChain network.

*Using the following invitation link for Cake DeFi, you will receive a $30 bonus paid in cryptocurrency DFI when you make an investment of at least $50: cakedefi.com/?ref=074201

DECENTRALIZED PREDICTION MARKETS

Prediction markets correspond to financial instruments that place bets on events in the future. These can be insurance, hedging products (e.g., options and futures), or bets on sports. Comparable to a decentralized stock exchange, one side provides liquidity in a pool. That side receives rewards in return. The other side places bets and wins or loses them. Pricing is based on the event's probability of occurring, as calculated by the users.

This can be illustrated more easily with a soccer bet as an example. Bets placed on the outcome of a soccer match have clear winners and losers (i.e,. no draw). Let's assume Bayern Munich is playing against Borussia Dortmund. 75% of the bets predict a win for Bayern Munich, while 25% bet on Dortmund. The possible profit for a Munich victory corresponds approximately to a factor of 1.33 [1/0.75 =1.33]. A victory of Dortmund corresponds to a factor of 4.00 [1/0.25=4.00] on the invested capital. A certain discount on the profit is made to pay out the rewards for the liquidity providers.

Comparable, albeit more complex, calculations take place for such bets in insurance and hedging. These are not yet sufficiently developed. Thus, they cannot report in detail on how they work today.

Their potential is enormous, however. Insurance and hedging have been almost exclusively confined to large institutions. With decentralization, private investors could benefit from rewards as liquidity providers. They can also take advantage of such insurance themselves. Another advantage over CeFi would be the achievement of fair pricing through market mechanisms. When events occur (e.g., insurance claims), the agreed sum is paid out immediately.

The selection of platforms for such services is currently still modest. Augur, for example, offers simple bets on sports events and price developments of cryptocurrencies. Unslashed Finance, on the other hand, offers insurance for smart contracts. Investors can participate and earn insurance premiums.

DEFI RISKS

When it comes to the risks of decentralized finance, clear distinctions need to be made. Essentially, dApps are based on the secure foundation of blockchain technology and smart contracts. This foundation allows transactions to be processed more reliably than in the traditional system. The Decentralized Value, Transfer, Lending, Tokenization and Prediction Markets use cases described are consistently reliable when programmed without errors. Nevertheless, investors should always have residual risks on the screen.

A practical approach for beginners is to limit oneself only to well-known decentralized applications. These usually enjoy higher confidence, as they have a longer history and have already won over many investors. On the homepage https://defillama.com/ you can find such a ranking, which is measured by the amount of the TVL score.

Exceptions confirm the rule:
The most recent example is the collapse of the Terra ecosystem along with its cryptocurrencies LUNA and UST. Terra's DeFi protocols were among the top 3 largest applications for a long time. However, in May 2022, an attack on an (economic) vulnerability in the system led to the cryptocurrencies being sold off. The technical implementation of the smart contracts worked flawlessly, but the cryptocurrencies lost trust and were hardly worth anything after the attack.

We assume that the developers of DeFi applications will learn from the mistakes of the past. Again, as an investor, it is important not to bet your entire fortune on a cryptocurrency or a DeFi application. The best strategy to avoid higher loss is still sufficient diversification.

Smart contract risk

Smart contracts ensure that contracts are executed properly and automatically. They remove the need for trust in human reliability. Ironically, these smart contracts are nevertheless programmed by humans. As a result, faulty codes pose a risk. Developers must be especially careful when dealing with more complex issues. With smart contracts, code is law. In 2016, for example, there was the well-known case of the blockchain project The DAO. A significant programming error in its smart contract led to the theft of 3.6 million ether. That was worth around $40 million at the time. It was a legal gray area because the hacker only exploited contractual loopholes.

Smart contracts are supported by additional auditing from external providers. This helps avoid errors in the future.
The best-known protocols in the DeFi area had to go through such audits. At the same time, dApps are usually open-source platforms. Thus, anyone with the appropriate programming know-how can access the code. These programmers can provide feedback for the developers. Additional incentives are created by bug bounty programs. Hackers are encouraged – even receiving rewards – to point out errors in the code. As a rule of thumb, two factors make a decentralized application more secure: the longer the platform has existed and the more assets are deposited on it (TVL score). Otherwise, hackers would have

incentive to hijack it through a gap in the smart contract.
Additionally, insurance policies compensating for smart
contract errors have even been offered. Such providers are
Nexus Mutual, Etherisc, and Unslashed Finance.

Scam risk

Decentralization enables a lot of freedom for its users. Thus, it
presupposes personal responsibility. However, this also attracts
creative scammers who steal the assets of naive users. For
example, they copy the design of legitimate websites and use a
slightly different spelling for the domain. If the user executes the
smart contract on the platform without taking a closer look at
the transaction details, the coins are lost and cannot be
reversed. In such cases, it is important to pay close attention to
the correct spelling of the web application.

Another example can be found on decentralized exchanges. In
some cases, users can list their own new coins. Scammers use
this ability to create so-called shitcoins, which resemble the
spelling of legitimate coins. The user may confuse a real Bitcoin
with the fake variant when exchanging. To avoid such cases, you
can enter the smart contract address of the token in the
exchange's search field instead of the abbreviation "BTC", e.g.
"0x2260FAC5E5542a773Aa44fBCfeDf7C193bc2C599"   (for
Wrapped Bitcoin on the Ethereum Blockchain). You can find the
official smart contract addresses for each blockchain at
EtherScan, PolygonScan, FTMScan etc. Additionally, most DEX
offer a filter for the selection of coins, which only selects
currencies from reputable sources.

Otherwise, the rule of thumb is to never give out the private key of your wallet (not even to a supposed customer service).

Risk of losing your wallet

In centralized exchanges, crypto assets are stored in an in-house online wallet. In contrast, with decentralized applications, the coins remain in your private wallet. The latter is considered a more secure option. Centralized crypto exchanges, despite improved security, still rely on trust rather than smart contracts. Though this is unlikely, the platform can be hacked overnight, disappear with its users' assets, or block them.

In the case of the private wallet, a distinction is made between two kinds of wallets. Software wallets such as MetaMask and hardware wallets such as the Ledger Nano*. These also have a certain residual risk. A software wallet can theoretically be hacked if a third party accesses the private key. This is accomplishable through a computer Trojan. A hardware wallet is comparable to cash or gold stored at home. It can be physically stolen, damaged, or lost. In both cases, however, you are responsible for your wallet. You are able to take the necessary security measures. Strong antivirus protection (for software wallets) or safe deposit boxes (for hardware wallets) can help.

*Use the following invitation link to go directly to the Ledger Wallet homepage to place a secure order for the Ledger Nano:
https://shop.ledger.com?r=34684ea950dc

Decrease in the value of cryptocurrencies

Every investor should be aware that cryptocurrencies can lose significant value to fiat currencies. Such a decline in value can even lead to a total loss. This is mainly due to cryptocurrencies being at the beginning of their development. No one can know how the crypto market will develop in the long term. Many different opinions lead to speculations about the future development of cryptocurrencies. This causes the prices to fluctuate enormously. This is especially true for coins that have not been on the market for long. It is a normal process, comparable to the internet stocks of the 90s. Those also showed high volatility in the beginning. The best companies, however, were able to establish themselves in the following years. Over time, their prices stabilized. This same development is noticeable in Bitcoin and Ethereum. Both already enjoy the trust of institutional investors. Their most turbulent times are likely behind them.

An exception to the risk of loss of value are stablecoins. They very rarely experience significant price fluctuations. If they do, it usually only lasts a short while. Viewed the other way around, stablecoins can suffer a loss in value compared to cryptocurrencies. This is due to corresponding fiat currencies having an inflationary character.

(Example 1)
Loss of value of Bitcoin: We have $60,000 and purchase 1 Bitcoin at the rate of $60,000/BTC. We now lend the Bitcoin on a decentralized lending platform, receiving 5% p.a. interest. After one year, we get back our Bitcoin + 0.05 Bitcoin in interest. However, at the same time, Bitcoin price has dropped to $50,000/BTC.

*Thus, our assets have shrunk to $52,500 [1.05 * $50,000 = $52,500]. We have suffered a loss of $7,500 although we received interest on the 1 Bitcoin.*

(Example 2)
Loss of value of USDC: We have $60,000 and exchange it for 60,000 USDC at a rate of 1:1. We lend the USDC at an interest rate of 10% p.a. After one year, we get back 66,000 USDC, including interest. We then exchange it again for fiat money (i.e., $66,000). At the same time, Bitcoin has risen from the original price of $60,000/BTC to $70,000/BTC. Consequently, despite the interest paid out on U.S. dollars, we have suffered a loss in value against Bitcoin.

Temporary increasing transaction costs

This sub-item is not directly a risk, but a cost item that we should keep in mind. Most DeFi applications are based on the Ethereum blockchain (ERC20). This network charges so-called **gas fees** for the settlement of transactions. If you send cryptocurrency from A to B, a small fee must always be deducted for the **validators**. The blockchain, in turn, is limited to a certain number of transactions per block. For Ethereum, this is usually generated about every 13 seconds. If demand increases, not all transactions can be deposited into the next blocks. They are prioritized, however, by the validators. This is done based on a financial incentive. It ensures the transactions with the highest gas fees flow first into the next block. They are thus processed the fastest. Your wallet provides an estimate of the gas fees for completing the transaction faster or slower.

Simple transactions like exchanging cryptocurrencies from A to B incurs relatively few gas fees. There are more complex transactions via smart contracts – e.g., for lending and liquidity mining. These, on the other hand, incur multiple and higher gas fees. In 2021, the fee for a simple transaction on the Ethereum blockchain was equal to about $10–20. For more complex transactions, it was equal to about $50–150. This is important when trying to generate interest income with smaller amounts on DeFi platforms. Fees may otherwise exceed the rewards.

The further development of Ethereum 2.0 is planned for 2022. This could, in turn, solve this problem, reducing transaction costs significantly. Alternatively, some DeFi platforms are already using much cheaper blockchains. These include Polygon, Avalanche, Fantom, and Binance Smart Chain. With them, transaction costs are mostly in the penny range.

Regulation and prohibition of DeFi

Cryptocurrencies (and DeFi in particular) are at risk of massive government interference. Regulators cannot completely shut down blockchain systems. They can, however, declare the use and possession of cryptocurrencies illegal. This would create a legal crime for the remaining users. Even if the crime was difficult to prove, it would still deter users. Additionally, the crypto ecosystem would lose all institutional investors. However, such a strict intervention in the economy could be met with resistance. Thus, measures weakening crypto will be more likely. There could be increased taxation on the capital gains of cryptocurrencies. Taxes could also rise on the interest generated via DeFi platforms.

Governments disapprove of DeFi's lack of KYC measures for identifying their customers. This creates a risk of dApps functioning for money laundering and other illegal transactions. However, it is questionable whether these regulatory measures are justified. They may only exist to prevent governments from losing their monopolies over money. The Crypto Crime Report by Chainalysis shows only a small degree of illegal activities. 0.34% of transactions on the crypto market can be attributed to illegal purposes. In the traditional financial system, this figure is over 2%.

Unpredictable risks

As in all parts of life, there are risks that we had not previously considered. Take the Corona crisis as an example. It occurred unexpectedly, ensuring that certain industries were severely set back. Conversely, other industries benefited from its outbreak. DeFi is still not sufficiently field-tested yet. While we see indications of its high potential, there are no guarantees of its future enforcement. It could also be that a new technology – even better than blockchain – will be invented.

Investors should always be aware of these risks and not put all their eggs in one basket. On the other hand, investors missing the DeFi trend could cause more damage. The current development shows that cryptocurrencies are becoming more and more important. The traditional financial system, however, is crumbling.

HOW TO EARN MONEY THROUGH DEFI

Now, let's get to the exciting part of the book. You're about to learn how to start generating passive income through DeFi. Basically, it is interest income you receive on your invested capital. This assumes that you already have assets that you put to work for you. With many dApps on the market, however, the entry hurdles are low. This means an investment with smaller amounts is already worthwhile.

The distribution yields are measured by the key figures APY and APR. APY stands for annual percentage yield and corresponds to the effective interest rate. This simulates a reinvestment of the regular payouts. This allows for the consideration of the compound interest effect. APR, on the other hand, stands for annual percentage rate. It is equivalent to the return without reinvestment or compound interest.

In addition to distribution yields, you will profit from increases in the value of cryptocurrencies. You must remember that large cryptocurrencies usually have lower growth rates. However, this is accompanied by a lower risk of loss. Conversely, smaller cryptocurrencies have higher growth potential. Likewise, these have a higher risk of loss. For example, Bitcoin has grown by about 60% in 2021. The more unknown coin **Terra** has grown by about 13,000%.

Below is a selection of concrete means of earning interest income with cryptocurrencies. Many of these services are not exclusively available through decentralized applications. In some cases, centrally organized companies offer suitable platforms. They may be considered reputable and even offer better conditions. Opinions differ on the issue of security. Decentralized providers strictly adhere to the smart contract and the blockchain. If something goes wrong with them, you cannot turn to the operator. Your coins would definitely be lost. However, your assets remain completely autonomous, so no third party can interfere. In the case of centralized platforms, you have the choice to turn to customer service. If there are errors in the smart contract, their insurance may compensate your loss. Their disadvantage is that your assets are stored on the provider's platform. Hence, you cannot freely dispose of them. In the worst-case scenario, your assets could be frozen, confiscated, or stolen. In the end, it's your decision. You can rely on pure DeFi platforms or compromise via central service providers.

FYI: The metrics you'll find in the following chapters can change quickly in the crypto space. My research for this book is based on current data as of December 2021.

PREPERATION

To take full advantage of DeFi applications, you must act on three key considerations.

Blockchain selection

DeFi applications can be handled by different blockchain systems. This is roughly comparable to Windows and MAC operating systems. Some applications are compatible across all systems. Others only work on one of the platforms. Similarly, not all cryptocurrencies can be exchanged on the same blockchain. The benchmark for the blockchain application of smart contracts is set by Ethereum. The associated ERC20 network enables the transfer of thousands of cryptocurrencies. Other well-known blockchain solutions are Binance Smart Chain, Polygon, Fantom, and Avalanche.

Wrapped tokens: Even on the most well-known blockchain networks, some important coins are not compatible. First and foremost, Bitcoin is incompatible because it operates exclusively on its own blockchain. Stablecoins were created to provide a solution for this. They allow such cryptocurrencies to be traded on several blockchain networks. These stablecoins replicate the value of other cryptocurrencies. The best known is the Wrapped Bitcoin (WBTC), which replicates the value of Bitcoin 1:1. For this, the company BitGo is committed to depositing one real Bitcoin for every single Wrapped Bitcoin on the market via an escrow agent. The new token enables Bitcoin to be transferred indirectly on other blockchains.

A decentralized variant without a trustee works via smart contracts. Let's look at an example using Cake DeFi. The original cryptocurrency (e.g., BTC) is securely deposited. Then, it is "frozen" on a wallet address in its original blockchain. Automatically, the smart contract creates a 1:1 copy of the cryptocurrency on a new blockchain. In this case, it creates a dBTC on the DeFiChain network. The wrapped token can then be traded as desired. If the user decides to convert the dBTC back into BTC, the process is executed in reverse. During this process, the generated wrapped token is burned again.

You may come across DeFi platforms that don't offer the blockchain on which your coins are deposited. You can then use so-called cross-chain bridges. Such platforms can be used to generate wrapped tokens for different networks. A well-known app for this is Anyswap.exchange. Note that this process can incur transaction fees in different amounts.

Blockchain transaction fees: Apart from coin compatibility, blockchain choice is important for avoiding higher transaction costs. Ethereum offers the most proven network, probably even with the highest security. However, it is very expensive due to high demand and currently low scalability. If you're not trading five-figure amounts, it's worth switching to an alternative. It's true that providers like Binance, Polygon, Fantom, and Avalanche are newer. Nevertheless, they are considered reputable and reliable. Their technologies were developed later, allowing them to compensate for Ethereum's weaknesses. Their big advantages are their speed and low fees.

As an example, ETH is traded against USDC on the wallet MetaMask. This platform transparently displays the transaction costs:

- Ethereum: approx. $50
- Binance: approx. $1.70
- Avalanche: approx. $0.40
- Polygon: approx. $0.05
- Fantom: approx. $0.007

Currently, Fantom and Polygon are the most affordable blockchain solutions. They are best suited for smaller amounts and frequent trades on DeFi platforms. However, this may change again over time. It's best to check the current transaction fees beforehand. Make sure you choose the right blockchain when transferring cryptocurrencies.

Another tip is that transaction fees can change depending on the time of day. At peak times, between 2 p.m. and 7 p.m. (CET), the costs are higher. During the quieter time, between 6 a.m. and 10 a.m. (CET), the fees are their lowest.

Wallet creation

In the DeFi area, you do not need to register. You do, however, need a wallet connected to the smart contract of a dApp. Here, you will find various providers of different software and hardware wallets. The best known and most supported application is MetaMask. It can be installed quickly via smartphone app or as a browser plugin. You can create unlimited wallets to store and transfer cryptocurrencies and execute smart contracts. It is important to choose a reliable password. Do not lose it under any circumstances. Otherwise, you will not be able to turn to anyone to recover the coins. It is also recommended you use a password manager such as **Keepass 2.0**. These allow you to centrally store your access to exchanges and wallets.

In the appendix of this book, you will find instructions for how to use Metamask.

Acquire cryptocurrencies on central exchanges

For DeFi applications, you currently have no choice but to use central exchanges. Only there you can deposit fiat money via bank transfer or credit card and swap it for cryptocurrencies. Afterwards, you are able to transfer these cryptocurrencies to your private wallet and trade on decentralized platforms. Conversely, you need to transfer cryptocurrencies from your wallet back to the central exchange to swap it for fiat money and wire it your bank account.

Recommended for this purpose is the platform Binance.* It is the largest, best-known crypto exchange with a daily trading volume over $25 billion. It offers just 0.1% trading fees and a selection of over 400 cryptocurrencies. Hardly any other exchange can match this offering. CoinMarketCap has praised Binance as the best crypto exchange, rating it 9.9 out of 10. It is followed by Coinbase, FTX, Kraken, and KuCoin. Unlike decentralized exchanges, Binance *is* subject to various regulations. Additionally, it verifies the identities of its users (KYC). Therefore, you must register officially. Your personal details will then be checked via photo identification.

*Use the following referral ID to get 5% discount for transactions on Binance: SXIL0YZL

Or use the invitation link directly:
https://www.binance.com/de/register?ref=SXIL0YZL

STAKING

The consensus mechanism within the blockchain is the technical basis enabling decentralized ecosystems. The validation process involves creating incentives for networks to manage themselves without central middlemen. Staking has emerged as an efficient way to do this in the DeFi world.

Proof of stake procedure

Staking is like mining for cryptocurrencies that use the proof of stake process as a consensus mechanism. Users pay fees to the network for transactions within the blockchain. To validate these transactions, the coins are deposited on a node in the blockchain for a certain period. A random process decides which node may add the next block and receive a commission financed by the accrued transaction costs. With some cryptocurrencies, additional coins are generated and distributed to the nodes. These are called **block rewards**. This incentivization temporarily ensures more users join the network, making it more stable.

Your stake is higher the more coins you deposit for the validation procedure. This increases the probability that you'll be selected in the random procedure, collecting the rewards. Consequently, with a smaller stake, you will be rarely selected.

Nevertheless, to enable regular earnings, participants can combine their coins in a staking pool. This is provided to a node, which takes care of the technical steps for the validation process. Then, the node distributes the rewards to all users. Smart contracts guarantee that coins are stored securely. They ensure that the income is allocated to their respective investors automatically. Therefore, you will receive regular interest. Such income will be paid out proportional to your invested capital.

This makes staking for investors comparable to a savings account. They can withdraw their coins at any time. However, it is also possible to "freeze" your coins. This allows you to deposit them in a staking pool for up to 10 years. With this method, you can secure higher interest rates for a longer period. However, until the time elapses, you have no access to your deposit. Sometimes, you can pay a fee to withdraw them earlier from the pool.

Staking is only possible for cryptocurrencies that use proof of stake consensus procedures. These include Cardano, Solana, and probably Ethereum in 2022. Coins such as Bitcoin, which use the proof of work method, cannot be staked as a result.

Staking

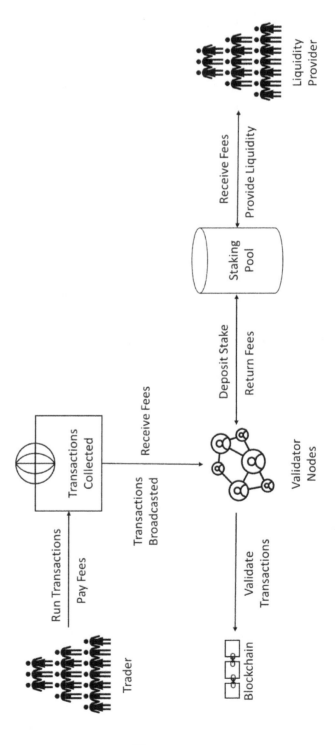

Staking rewards

Staking rewards depend on two factors:

1. How often is the cryptocurrency transferred, incurring transaction fees? The higher the activity, the higher the absolute volume of fees collected. Such fees can then be distributed to the validators.

2. What is the volume of coins provided by the nodes for the validation process? The more investors participate in staking and deposit coins, the lower their rewards. Consequently, they must share the transaction fees with more users. This is why their profit share decreases.

(Example 1): For the cryptocurrency Cardano (ADA), a total of 1,000 coins are staked by all validators. The annual reward is 100 ADA coins. These coins are distributed equally among the validators. So, everyone has a return of 10% p.a. [100 ADA Rewards/1,000 ADA Stake = 10%]. Possible increases in value are not considered in this return indicator.

(Example 2): Let's assume that the transaction frequency remains the same, but more investors join. These investors deposit an additional 4,000 ADA in the staking pool. This leaves a total reward of 100 ADA per year distributed among more participants. In this case, their respective return is reduced to 2.5% p.a.

(Example 3): 5,000 ADA are still deposited in the staking pool, but the cryptocurrency is traded more frequently. Thus, the generated transaction costs increase to 200 ADA per year. This increases the investors' return to 4% p.a.

More well-known cryptocurrencies logically have more users and liquidity. As a result, their percentage staking returns are lower. For the top five largest staking coins, the rewards are around 5–10% p.a.

Example:
- Ethereum 2.0: ~5%
- Cardano: ~5%
- Solana: ~6%

If you want higher returns, you must resort to coins with less deposited liquidity. Reasonably solid cryptocurrencies within the Top 100 commonly have returns of 50–200%.

Example:
- DeFiChain: ~60%
- PancakeSwap: ~75%
- Axie Infinity: ~115%

If you want to take even higher risk, look at recently issued coins outside the Top 2,000. In this case, rewards of more than 5,000% p.a. are possible.

Example:
- OlympusDAO: ~7,000%
- ClimateDAO: ~42,000
- Wonderland: ~73,000%

However, the more unknown cryptocurrencies are subject to higher risks of price fluctuation. You may significantly increase the number of coins, but the cryptocurrency itself could lose value. This results in a loss afterwards.

Staking provider

In staking, you can use the process to generate passive income in four ways. The first two methods require low effort, initiated with the push of a button. For the other two methods, you need more initiative and technical know-how.

Staking on dApps: Some developers allow you to stake their in-house cryptocurrency on their web or smartphone app. The application is simple. You connect your wallet with the app and confirm the smart contract. This deposits your coins in the staking pool, and you receive regular payouts. Well-known platforms that enable this method include PancakeSwap (CAKE), Axie Infinity (AXIS), and Cake DeFi (DFI).

Detailed instructions for this procedure can be found in the appendix of this book.

Staking on central exchanges: Larger central crypto exchanges offer the option to stake the coins that are stored in your account. The method is convenient since most users leave their cryptocurrencies on these accounts anyway and can now generate passive income as well. For the application, you confirm which of your coins you want to stake and then receive regular payouts. The most popular exchanges for this are Binance, Kraken, and BlockFi.

Detailed instructions for this procedure can be found in the appendix of this book.

Staking as a service: With staking as a service, you provide your coins to a larger node via a smart contract. It takes over the technical part, deducting a small fee. Then, it distributes the rewards to you proportionally. For this process, you need a special wallet where you can nominate the validator. Well-known providers for staking as a service are Everstake, Infstone, and Chorus One.

Independent staking: You operate your own node, validate transactions, and profit directly from blockchain rewards. You can find instructions on the homepage of the corresponding cryptocurrency. This procedure is not suitable for most users due to the technical complexity alone. Because of that, we will not go into more detail.

LENDING

Lending allows you to grant your cryptocurrencies as a loan. In return, you'll receive interest. The positive thing on the lender's side is that the loan amount is secured by collateral. This means that the probability of default is very low. Other risks have already been discussed in the subsection on lending risk.

As a borrower, you can also earn money despite interest payments. This is achievable by shorting the borrowed currency or investing in another cryptocurrency with leverage.

Lending rewards

Depending on the cryptocurrency, the rewards for lending may differ. The interest rates lean on supply (how many coins are offered by lenders) and demand (how many coins are demanded by borrowers). The interest rates are subject to change at any time. This also considers the volatility of the coin. More precisely, it involves the expected probability that it will increase or decrease in value. For cryptocurrencies with more risk, the lending interest rate is correspondingly higher. This is because many borrowers also try to short this coin through loans.

For very popular cryptocurrencies, lending interest rates are paid out between 2–10%.

Example:
- Bitcoin: ~5%
- Ethereum: ~5%
- Binance: ~6%
- Polkadot: ~9%

Fun Fact: U.S. dollar stablecoins have higher interest rates than Bitcoin and Ethereum. This occurs because the community expects inflation and, thus, higher depreciation of fiat currencies. Some coins like USDC, USDT, and DAI are reaching interest rates above 10% per year.

Some do not want to invest in volatile cryptocurrencies. For them, lending dollar stablecoins is a better source of income than traditional savings accounts.

Example:
- USDC: 8%
- DAI: 8.5%
- USDT: 10%

In rarer cases, lesser-known cryptocurrencies can also earn interest rates above 10%.

Example:
- SushiSwap: ~21%
- Maker: ~36.5%
- Tron: ~44%

Lending provider

Compared to staking, lending is significantly more flexible in terms of cryptocurrency options. Pretty much any cryptocurrency can be lent. Accordingly, the number of providers for this service is also larger.

When it comes to lending, you can use centralized and decentralized service providers. They differ in terms of the following criteria:

- Cryptocurrency selection
- Amount of interest
- Amount of collateral deposited (LTV)
- Maturities
- Frequency of profit distributions

Central lending provider

The most popular lending providers on centralized platforms are:

- Nexo*
- BlockFi
- Crypto.com
- Celsius Network
- Binance

One of the leading platforms is Nexo* with over 2.5 million users. The provider manages $13 billion in assets. It is currently regulated by authorities in Switzerland and Estonia.

On Nexo, you can borrow over 40 different fiat currencies or stablecoins. You can deposit 22 different cryptocurrencies as collateral. The average is an LTV of 0.5. If the LTV rises above 0.714, a margin call reminds the borrower to increase the collateral or partially repay the loan amount. When the LTV exceeds 0.833, the collateral is liquidated. Another interesting feature concerns fiat money (e.g., euros, dollars, and British pounds). It can be deposited directly to earn around 4–12% interest, even without cryptocurrencies. The rewards are partially distributed by the in-house Nexo token.

Compared to other platforms, Nexo is clearly in the upper range of average lending rewards. Thanks to BitGo and Ledger insurance policies, investors' assets are secured for up to $375 million. User surveys on platforms such as Trustpilot also show positive customer experiences.

To lend on Nexo, users must register with an ID card/passport. They can then purchase cryptocurrencies with fiat money directly through the platform. Users can then lend them to earn interest. Detailed instructions for this procedure can be found in the appendix of this book.

*Using the following invitation link, you will receive an additional $25 bonus in Bitcoin on Nexo: https://t1p.de/1iymj

Decentralized lending provider

Some of the best-known decentralized lending providers include:

- Aave
- Compound
- MakerDao
- InstaDApp

Aave is currently the third-largest DeFi app, with a total value locked of $14 billion. Aave is based solely on smart contracts, which its users can access via the web. New users do not need to register, simply connecting their wallets with the platform. Aave is thus unregulated, with no central management or customer service. However, the network has access to the programming code on Github. It exchanges information on various forums or Telegram groups.

Currently, only tokens running on the Ethereum, Polygon, or Avalanche blockchain can be lent on Aave. The amount of collateral deposited differs depending on the cryptocurrency. On average, the LTV ratio is 0.8. There is no margin call on Aave. Collaterals are automatically liquidated once the liquidation threshold is exceeded. In return, users can borrow an unlimited amount of capital. They are not bound to a fixed term for loan repayment. As a rule, interest rates are variable. If the borrower prefers a fixed interest rate, this can also be granted at a premium.

Detailed instructions for this procedure can be found in the appendix of this book.

LIQUIDITY MINING

Liquidity mining enables the swapping of cryptocurrencies on decentralized exchanges. Liquidity providers deposit at least one currency pair in a pool and receive rewards in return. This could be, for example, USDC and ETH with a value ratio of 50:50. Traders can then demand the coins from the pool by exchanging USDC for ETH or vice versa. The trade results in transaction costs.

Liquidity mining rewards

On average, the highest returns in the DeFi area can be achieved via liquidity mining. Rewards are distributed in the form of **LP tokens**. This is technically a new cryptocurrency representing a claim on the proceeds of liquidity pools via smart contract. LP tokens can consequently be exchanged for cryptocurrencies submitted in liquidity mining. In this process, the LP token is burned from the blockchain. Alternatively, LP tokens can be traded on decentralized exchanges against completely different cryptocurrencies. They can be also staked to generate even higher interests (see later sections on *yield farming*).

Liquidity mining rewards are basically equal to the transaction costs collected on the DEX. In many cases, additional block rewards are distributed to provide higher incentives. This temporarily provides more liquidity. The block rewards are created by issuing more of the in-house token. In addition, the interest rates are always variable. They can change significantly from one day to the next. The rates depend on how much liquidity is offered for the currency pair. They are also affected by how often they are swapped on the DEX. Suppose there are fewer liquidity providers for the currency pair in the market. Then, the remaining LPs will receive a higher share of the transaction costs. Increasing demand for the currency pair also has a positive effect.

It consequently generates more transaction costs and distributes them to the pool. Conversely, the rewards decrease if there is more liquidity and/or the currency pair is traded less.

Supply and demand for the currency pair mostly depend on their volatility and correlation (see: *impermanent loss* in the following chapter). For currency pairs with less volatility, growing almost evenly with each other, the rewards are 5–25% p.a.

Example:
- Bitcoin/Ethereum Pool: ~6%
- Binance/Bitcoin Pool: ~18%
- Cardano/Binance Pool: ~22%

A currency pair with high volatility or low correlation means the probability of a loss in value is significantly higher. This includes pools that combine a cryptocurrency and a fiat currency (in the form of a stablecoin). An example of one such combination is Ethereum and USDC. Due to the increased risk, the liquidity pool for the currency pair is significantly smaller. However, it potentially generates more returns. In some cases, such currencies achieve interest rates over 25% per year.

Example:
- Ethereum/USDC Pool: ~25%
- Binance (BNB)/Binance USD (BUSD) Pool: 43%
- DefiChain/Bitcoin Pool: 103%.

Pools that have recently been launched are particularly interesting for high returns. For example, DefiChain allows users to conduct liquidity mining for tokenized shares. A pool of the stablecoin dUSD and a tokenized Tesla share initially saw returns of over 300%. However, these pools are usually quickly filled with liquidity by investors. Thus, the high rewards only apply in the short term.

For risk-averse investors, liquidity pools with two stablecoins are a good choice. The currency pair USDC and USDT, for example, generates rewards of ~9% per year. Thus, the return is significantly higher than in the traditional financial sector. Additionally, it is generated to be almost risk-free.

Impermanent loss

In liquidity mining, the risk of impermanent loss should not be neglected. It occurs more often with volatile currency pairs that do not correlate with each other. Impermanent loss is equivalent to profit lost by depositing the two cryptocurrencies into a liquidity pool. This can be avoided by simply keeping them in your wallet. The risk occurs when one of the coins in the pair suffers a significant price change. Thus, the original ratio of both coins has changed.

The following example can illustrate this mathematical loss.

We want to deposit $10,000 in the form of 1 ETH and 5,000 USDC into a liquidity pool. The exchange rate is therefore 1 ETH = 5,000 USDC and the deposit ratio is 50:50. In addition, there were a total of 9 ETH and 45,000 USDC in the previous pool. They were funded by other LPs. Due to our additional liquidity contribution, we have a 10% share of the total pool.

Impermanent Loss

State 1: ETH Price = 5,000 USDC

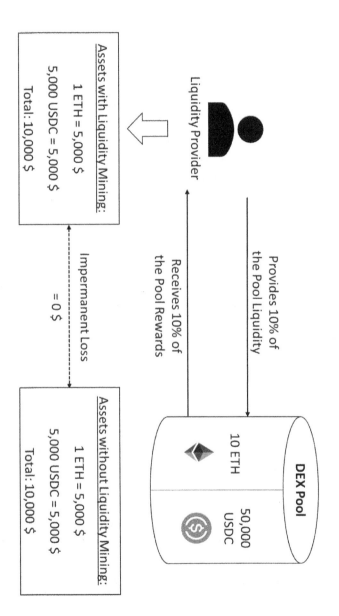

DEX Pool

10 ETH
50,000 USDC

Liquidity Provider

Provides 10% of
the Pool Liquidity

Receives 10% of
the Pool Rewards

Assets with Liquidity Mining:

1 ETH = 5,000 $
5,000 USDC = 5,000 $
Total: 10,000 $

Assets without Liquidity Mining:

1 ETH = 5,000 $
5,000 USDC = 5,000 $
Total: 10,000 $

Impermanent Loss

= 0 $

Suppose the general market price for 1 ETH increases from 5,000 USDC to 20,000 USDC. As this happens, arbitrage traders add USDC to the pool. In turn, they remove ETH until the ratio reflects the correct price. This keeps the volume of liquidity in the pool constant. It does, however, change the ratio of assets. For example, suppose we want the DEX to reach the new exchange rate of 20,000 USDC/ETH. The liquidity pool must then realize a total composition of 5 ETH and 100,000 USDC.

We now decide to withdraw our currency pair from the liquidity pool again. We are still entitled to a share of 10% of the pool. To simplify this example, we'll ignore all rewards generated by transaction costs for the LP providers. So, our payout is 0.5 ETH and 10,000 USDC, for a total value of $20,000. This sounds like a very good return at first. After all, we have practically doubled our investment. But what would have happened if we had not done any liquidity mining and kept our coins in the wallet? In that case, we would own 1 ETH and 5,000 USDC. That's a total value of $25,000, as the ETH rate has risen to 20,000 USDC/ETH. The difference of 5,000 USDC is thus our impermanent loss.

Impermanent Loss

State 2: ETH Price increases to 20,000 USDC

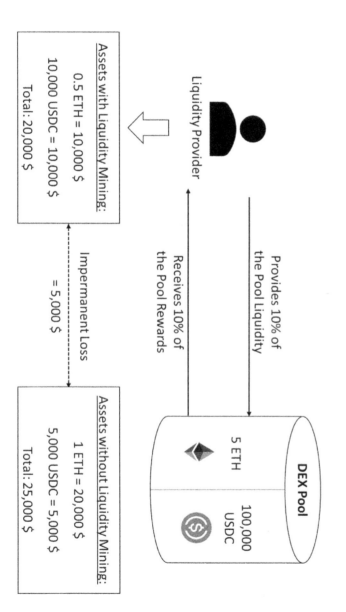

Liquidity Provider

Provides 10% of the Pool Liquidity

Receives 10% of the Pool Rewards

DEX Pool

5 ETH | 100,000 USDC

Assets with Liquidity Mining:

0.5 ETH = 10,000 $

10,000 USDC = 10,000 $

Total: 20,000 $

Impermanent Loss

= 5,000 $

Assets without Liquidity Mining:

1 ETH = 20,000 $

5,000 USDC = 5,000 $

Total: 25,000 $

Fortunately, impermanent loss is only significant with substantial price fluctuations, like the above example. If the exchange rates differ by only 25%, the impermanent loss is less than 1%. What follows is an overview of the impermanent loss for each exchange rate change:

Price Fluctuation	Impermanent Loss
25%	0.6%
50%	2%
75%	3.8%
100%	5.7%
200%	13.4%
300%	20%
400%	25.5%

The impermanent loss only becomes permanent when coins are sold during the price fluctuation. If the coins remain in the pool, it is possible for the prices to recover again. They can still reach the original ratio. At the same time, the impermanent loss is compensated by the liquidity mining rewards. Arbitrageurs trying to rebalance the price cause further transaction costs to flow to the LPs. This is due to increased trading. Liquidity mining can be worthwhile despite significant price changes. In the example above, they result in an impermanent loss of 20%. Such a loss is due to a four-fold change in the USDC/ETH currency pair. Suppose the rewards for the currency pair were, for example, 25% in the same period. We would still be in the plus with 5% [25% rewards – 20% impermanent loss = 5% return].

The risk for impermanent loss can be minimized by depositing two strongly positively correlated or stable cryptocurrencies (e.g., dollar stablecoins) in the pool.

Liquidity mining provider

Liquidity mining is offered exclusively on decentralized exchanges. There is no platform offering ideal conditions across the board for all known currency pairs. This is especially true regarding the amount of rewards. It is therefore worthwhile to use several platforms at the same time. Then, you can compare them for the desired currency pair. The best-known providers for liquidity mining are:

- PancakeSwap
- Balancer
- Uniswap
- SushiSwap
- Curve Finance
- DeFiChain/CakeDefi

With a TVL of $13 billion, PancakeSwap is one of the largest decentralized applications. Originally, the CAKE token was created from a fork of the SushiSwap protocol, which is, in turn, a fork of the decentralized exchange UniSwap. This spin-off derives from slow transaction speeds and high transaction costs over the Ethereum blockchain. PancakeSwap relies instead on the Binance Smart Chain, which currently enables much more efficient transactions. With liquidity mining on PancakeSwap, LPs receive the in-house governance token, CAKE. Among other things, a governance token grants its holders voting rights for future decisions. These include determining how high trading fees should be on the DEX. The CAKE token has a market capitalization of nearly $5 billion. This value places it among the Top 50 largest cryptocurrencies.

Moreover, PancakeSwap is clearly structured. This ensures the offered currency pairs and expected rewards can be found easily. A tutorial for liquidity mining using PancakeSwap can be found in the appendix of this book.

Another platform worth mentioning is Balancer. It offers liquidity mining on several blockchains. The platform allows more than two currency pairs as well as asymmetric deposits (e.g., 80:20 instead of 50:50). For all LPs that only rely on stablecoins, Balancer offers the currency quartet USDC/USDT/DAI/TUSD. On this quartet, a return of about 20% is paid.

YIELD FARMING

Yield farming refers to a strategy of moving your cryptocurrencies between interest-generating DeFi platforms. The goal is to shift them back and forth, resulting in the highest possible returns. Basically, it involves the revenue streams from staking, lending, and liquidity mining. This revenue can optionally be boosted by leverage. However, unlike the methods mentioned so far, yield farming is an active process. It requires more effort and risk-taking. "Farmers" must always keep an eye on interest rates and price changes of cryptocurrencies. If the rewards on one platform deteriorate, the coins are withdrawn from the pool. Then, they are deposited on another application with higher interest rates.

An additional incentive is created by decentralized platforms that are still in their early stages. Still fledgling, they often try to attract more users and liquidity. In addition to the usual income from transaction costs, they reward farmers with more tokens. This depends on how early you start yield farming a new currency and the height of your risk tolerance. Returns over 10,000% p.a. can sometimes be achieved. The high rewards, however, rarely last for a long time.

With yield farming, we go deeper into the field of DeFi. In the appendix of this book, you will find two different yield farming tutorials.

DEFI ARBITRAGE

Investments usually work in such a way that products increase in value after a certain period. We take risks where we hope that our investments eventually increase in price. In an arbitrage transaction, however, it is not the time difference that matters but the place difference. Arbitrage is therefore a risk-free way to profit from deviations in rates or prices across platforms. For example, let's say a product is traded on Exchange A at the price of $10. The same product is traded on Exchange B at the price of $12. Therefore, an arbitrageur buys from Exchange A and immediately sells on Exchange B. You would then make a $2 profit. Theoretically, there is no risk involved if the trade is completed without delay. Profitable arbitrage is possible when markets are not yet fully efficient. In the young, still developing DeFi area, this is often the case. This allows various price differences to be exploited.

Anyone who wants to engage in arbitrage should be aware that this also represents an active investment. Thus, it requires more effort, market know-how, and programming skills. In the following sections, I will only explain the basics and potentials. For more details, you can seek out various websites and YouTube tutorials.

Price arbitrage

Decentralized exchanges operate according to an automated market maker. This AMM calculates the exchange rate for a currency pair based on liquidity. The ratio of the two currencies becomes unbalanced more often on a smaller DEX. This causes prices to deviate significantly compared to more liquid exchanges.

The price of the cryptocurrency Chainlink (LINK) is 34.16 USDC on Balancer's decentralized exchange. At the same time, the coin is traded on Binance's central exchange for about 36.40 USDC. For a quick arbitrage trade, you could purchase more of the LINK token via Balancer. Then, you'd transfer it to your Binance wallet and sell it there. This results in a profit of 2.24 USDC each.

This example doesn't consider the order fees of the respective exchange and the transaction costs. You should take these into account, as they decide whether your arbitrage business will be profitable. Professionals in this business also combine arbitrage business with so-called flash loans. These are very short-term, unsecured loans via lending platforms. Their arbitrageurs use additional leverage to trade higher amounts.

Interest arbitrage

The second option is to exploit different interest rates on lending platforms. This is only partially arbitrage, as you still rely on the time component for a profit. For interest arbitrage, you borrow a cryptocurrency on one platform at a low interest rate. Then, you invest it again at a higher interest rate on another platform.

For example, on the <u>Oasis app</u>, you can deposit $10,000 in Ethereum as collateral (LTV = 0.60). This allows you to borrow about 6,000 DAI (equivalent to 6,000 U.S. dollars). This loan currently has an interest rate of 0.5%. You can reinvest these 6,000 DAI on a central platform like <u>Nexo</u>* with a current interest rate of 8%. This will lead to you receiving approximately 480 DAI in rewards at the end of the year. From this, you settle the interest on the Oasis app to the tune of about 30 DAI. Consequently, you've made a profit of $450, representing 4.5% of your original ether coins. The added benefit is that you didn't have to sell your ether and pay taxes on it.

Note that the interest rate on this arbitrage deal can change at any time. This could make the deal unprofitable. In that case, you can simply pay off the loan on both sides. This is another place where you must consider transaction costs.

CONCLUSION

DeFi has the potential to turn the traditional financial world completely upside down. It could redefine the system. Money is no longer controlled by financial institutions and states but by the people themselves. The blockchain makes it possible to display all structures transparently. This ensures that everyone knows what they are getting into. It also shows them the fees they must pay and how they can participate in the system.

The DeFi world is still young, however. We have no certainty yet that the concept will prevail. In any case, there will be resistance from anyone wanting to preserve the current financial system. They will want to continue profiting from it unilaterally. However, decentralized applications are globally widespread. They cannot be wiped out at the push of a button. So, in the end, both systems may exist parallel to each other.

It's true that DeFi has some difficulties regarding the linking of digital and analog worlds. These applications, however, can already deliver high added value today. For you as an investor, this represents an opportunity. You can enter the early phase of a technology cycle and benefit from the high returns.

CLOSING WORDS

"The reason people think DeFi is so complicated is because we never had to understand finance before. That's how banks scammed us so easily."

- Reddit: Mandrake_m2 -

DeFi has been a niche until now, understood by only a few users. With this book, I hope that you can take embrace its insights and spread them. Get involved in revolutionizing the existing worn-out financial system. Contribute to the creation of a better world. Please recommend this book to anyone interested in cryptocurrencies, investments, and passive income. Please also write a review on Amazon to help spread the word.

Good luck in the new monetary system!

APPENDIX

Tutorial: MetaMask Wallet

- On the start page of the wallet, you will see your public key. Enter this code to receive coins from another wallet or from a crypto exchange.

- In *Settings/Security & Privacy*, you can create a backup password of random combined words. You should use this option. Write the backup password down on a piece of paper. Be sure to store the paper in a safe place.

- You can add an additional blockchain via *Settings/Networks*. By default, the Ethereum network is programmed in. If you want to transact via another blockchain, you can determine the data needed to add a new network.

- Depending on the cryptocurrency, it may not be immediately displayed in your wallet. In this case, you can import more tokens via the wallet's start page. An internet search will help you enter the correct data to add the coin.

- MetaMask estimates the transaction costs (gas fees) of transferring coins or executing smart contracts. Here you can adjust your preference – fast, standard, or slow execution.

- MetaMask offers an interface to exchange cryptocurrencies directly via decentralized exchanges. However, the operator charges an additional fee of 0.875%.

- If MetaMask does not connect to a dApp from your smartphone, try connecting from your desktop. Use Google Chrome and the MetaMask browser plugin.

Tutorial: Decentralized Exchange

Here's how to use decentralized exchanges to swap cryptocurrencies with UniSwap. In this example, we will exchange ETH for DAI.

1. Go to the platform https://app.uniswap.org and connect your wallet – e.g., MetaMask – with the application (button on the top right).

2.. If necessary, adjust the blockchain on which the transaction is to be executed. Currently, UniSwap works on the Ethereum, Polygon, Arbitrum, and Optimism networks.

3. Select the *Swap* menu item and select the currency pair you want to exchange with each other. In the input field above, add the amount you want to deposit (e.g., 1 ETH). You will get an automatic calculation of how much you would receive from the other currency (in this case, 3,158.09 DAI).

4. With the gear above, you can adjust the Slippage Tolerance and the Transaction Deadline.

5. Confirm the transaction by clicking the *Swap* button.

6. Confirm the smart contract transaction on your wallet. This process will incur transaction costs. After a brief time, the exchanged cryptocurrency is credited to your wallet.

Tutorial: Tokenization

Using Mirror Finance, I will explain how you can issue, for example, a Tesla share. Mirror is based on the Terra blockchain (LUNA). You can use the blockchain on the Terra Station wallet. You also need a cryptocurrency compatible with this network. For example, you can purchase the stablecoin **UST** on Binance and transfer it to your wallet.

1. Visit the homepage at https://mirrorprotocol.app and connect your wallet to the application. Here, you use the Terra network.

2. Select the *Borrow* menu item. You will get an overview of the different assets you can tokenize.

2.1 The Terraswap Price shows you the price at which the asset is traded on the Terra decentralized exchange.

2.2 The Oracle Price corresponds to the average price traded on central exchanges. This is the price at which your dToken is issued via smart contract.

2.3 The premium is calculated by the percentage deviation of the DEX and Oracle price. As a rule, the DEX price is somewhat higher. This is because demand for dTokens on decentralized exchanges is currently very high.

2.4 The Minimum Collateral Ratio indicates the minimum collateral deposited to tokenize the asset.

3. Select the desired asset – e.g., Tesla stock (mTSLA).

4. In Point 1, select the cryptocurrency and the amount you want to deposit as collateral – e.g., 1,000 UST.

5. Select the desired collateral ratio in Point 2. For the Tesla share, you must deposit at least 150% of the value by UST. Mirror recommends depositing at least 200% or more. This way, you avoid your collateral possibly liquidating due to occasional price fluctuations.

6. Point 3 shows how many tokenized Tesla shares should be credited to your wallet.

7. Confirm the operation by clicking the *Borrow* button.

8. Confirm the smart contract transaction via your wallet. Transaction costs are incurred here.

9. After a few seconds or minutes, the tokenized share will be credited to your wallet.

10. You can then exchange the tokenized share via the Trade menu item. Alternatively, you can generate interest by providing your share from the Farm menu item.

Update May 2022:
After the crash of the Terra ecosystem, this approach may no longer be current. At this time, it is not yet determined how the Mirror Protocol will work. Until then, I recommend using an alternative like DeFiChain.

Tutorial: Staking

Below is a tutorial for staking using the cryptocurrency CAKE as an example. The token can be staked on the decentralized exchange of PancakeSwap. Additionally, it can be staked on the central exchange of Binance. The respective methods can also be applied to other cryptocurrencies.

Staking on PancakeSwap

1. Visit the homepage at https://pancakeswap.finance and connect your wallet to the application. Here, you use the Binance Smart Chain network.

2. Select the *Earn/Pool* menu item. You will receive an overview of the different tokens you can deposit for staking. The key figures – APY and APR – show the expected returns.

3. For this example, select the *Manual CAKE* or *Auto CAKE* function. The latter allows your rewards to be automatically reinvested, generating compound interest.

4. Select the number of CAKE tokens you want to deposit and confirm the process by clicking the *Enable* button.

5. Confirm the smart contract transaction via your wallet. Transaction costs are incurred here.

6. After a few seconds or minutes, the transaction is completed.

Staking on Binance

1. Visit the homepage at https://www.binance.com/de/register?ref=28390658 (affiliate link)

2. Register or log in to your account.

3. Go to the *Earn/Staking* menu item.

4. You will receive an overview of the different tokens you can deposit for staking. The key figure *Est. APY* shows the expected return.

5. For this example, select the cryptocurrency CAKE. Decide whether you want to stake for 30, 60, or 90 days. The duration may change the yield.

6. Click on the *Stake Now* button.

7. Select the number of CAKE tokens you want to deposit.

8. Confirm you have read the Terms of Use, and click the *Confirm* button.

9. The staking rewards will then be paid out to your online wallet. After the term ends, you can repeat the process as much as you like.

Tutorial: Lending

This tutorial explains how lending is applied centrally and decentrally through Nexo and Aave. We consider the situation of the lender wanting to generate interest income. In this example, we will lend the crypto currency Polygon (MATIC token).

Lending on Aave

1. Visit the homepage at https://app.aave.com.

2. Connect your wallet to the app.

3. Switch the network to the Polygon blockchain.

4. Select the *Deposit* menu item.

5. You will receive an overview of the different tokens you can deposit for lending. The key figure *APY* shows you the expected return in the currency of the lent token. In addition, Aave pays block rewards in some cases (see indicator in the rectangle).

6. In this example, click on the cryptocurrency MATIC.

7. The new window provides an overview of various key figures for lending the cryptocurrency. Among other things, these show the collateralization ratios for the borrowers. As lenders, these values are uninteresting, as sufficient collateral is guaranteed for all currencies.

8. Select the number of MATIC tokens you want to deposit.

9. Confirm the process by clicking the *Continue* button. In the new window, click *Deposit.*

10. Confirm the smart contract transaction via your wallet. Transaction costs are incurred here.

11. After a few seconds or minutes, the transaction is completed.

12. The menu item *My Dashboard* gives an overview of your awarded tokens and rewards.

13. You can then use your deposit as collateral and borrow other cryptocurrencies. To do so, go to the menu item *Borrow* and follow the instructions.

Lending on Nexo

To use services on Nexo, you first have to register on the platform. With your ID card, you will be able to verify yourself. You can then buy cryptocurrencies directly on Nexo using fiat money. Additionally, you can transfer existing coins to the online wallet.

1. Visit the homepage at https://t1p.de/1iymj (affiliate link).

2. The homepage provides an overview of your cryptocurrencies stored on the online wallet. If necessary, you can transfer more coins to your Nexo wallet. Just click the *Top Up* button. Your deposit address will be displayed in the new window.

3. All cryptocurrencies deposited in the Nexo wallet receive an interest rate. This rate currently ranges from 4–10%.

4. Optionally, you can generate additional rewards via the green button. Click to reveal the interest statement ("Earning up to x%").

4.1 One option is to freeze your coin for a period of 30 days. To do this, select the desired amount and confirm the process.

4.2 The second option is to purchase Nexo tokens. This allows you to participate in the loyalty program. Plus, you will benefit from higher interest rates.

5. You can then use your deposit as collateral, borrowing other cryptocurrencies. Nexo displays a credit line on the homepage.

Tutorial: Liquidity Mining

Before you start liquidity mining, make sure you have both cryptocurrencies in your wallet. In this example, we provide liquidity for the currency pair BNB and CAKE. There must be a 1:1 ratio based on the DEX price. If necessary, you can adjust this balance. Just swap BNB for CAKE (or vice versa) on the exchange beforehand.

1. Visit the homepage at https://pancakeswap.finance.

2. Connect your wallet to the application. Here, you use the Binance Smart Chain network.

3. Switch to the *Trade/Liquidity* menu item.

4. Click the *Add Liquidity* button.

5. Select the tokens in the new window – for this example, BNB and CAKE.

6. Adjust the amount to be deposited in one of the two currencies. You will automatically see how many tokens you need to deposit from the other currency pair.

7. Click the *Supply* button and then *Confirm Supply.*

8. Confirm the smart contract transaction via your wallet. Transaction costs are incurred here. From now on, you will receive a share of the transaction costs collected via this currency pair.

9. To generate additional rewards, switch to the *Earn/Farms* menu item.

10. Here, you get an overview of all currency pairs currently eligible for liquidity mining. In addition, *PancakeSwap* pays further block rewards in the form of CAKE tokens in various amounts. The expected return can be found in the APR column.

11. In this example, you select the CAKE-BNB currency pair.

12. Confirm the process by clicking the *Enable* button.

13. Confirm the smart contract transaction via your wallet. Transaction costs are incurred here.

14. In the same window, you will see your deposited currency pairs and rewards.

Tutorial: Yield Farming

Yield Farming Strategy: PancakeSwap

On PancakeSwap, the yield farming strategy is much easier. However, you bear the risk of possible losses in cryptocurrency value. The idea combines liquidity mining and the subsequent staking of the rewards – i.e., the LP tokens. In the example, we again use the combination of the BNB and CAKE tokens (see *Liquidity Mining* and *Staking Tutorial*).

1. Visit the homepage at https://pancakeswap.finance.

2. Connect your wallet to the application. Here, you use the Binance Smart Chain network.

3. Switch to the *Trade/Liquidity* menu item.

4. Click the *Add Liquidity* button.

5. In the new window, select the tokens BNB and CAKE for this example.

6. Adjust the amount to be deposited in one of the two currencies. You will automatically see how many tokens you must deposit from the other currency.

7. Click the *Supply* button and then *Confirm Supply.*

8. Confirm the smart contract transaction via your wallet. Transaction costs are incurred here.

9. Switch to the *Earn/Farms* menu item.

10. Select the currency pair – CAKE-BNB, for this example.

11. Confirm the process by clicking the *Enable* button.

12. Confirm the smart contract transaction via your wallet. Transaction costs are incurred here.

FYI: From this point onwards, rewards of approximately 42% are currently paid out for liquidity mining.

13. Switch to the *Earn/Pool* menu item.

14. For this example, select the *Auto CAKE* function and click *Enable*

15. Confirm the smart contract transaction via your wallet. Transaction costs are incurred here.

FYI: By restaking CAKE LP tokens, you will receive an additional return. Currently, this return is about 65% based on your rewards.

Yield Farming

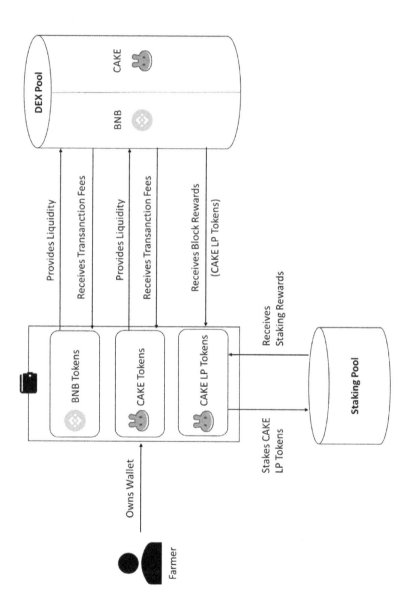

Yield Farming Strategy: Wonderland

The Wonderland platform advertises a type of stablecoin backed by cryptocurrencies, among other things. Since the project has only existed since fall of 2021, they currently offering a fabulous return of over 80,000% annually. The rewards are generated by staking the associated TIME token. However, the cryptocurrency should be used with a high degree of caution since the business model might fail. Such breakdown could lead to a total loss. It's also possible for the coin to remain reasonably stable. In this case, you will multiply your investment after a short time.

Since Wonderland functions on the Avalanche blockchain, it is a good idea to acquire the TIME token by swapping against AVAX coins.

1. Buy any amount of the cryptocurrency Avalanche (AVAX) on any exchange. Binance is the best choice here for the reasons already mentioned.

2. Transfer AVAX to your wallet.

3. Visit the homepage at https://traderjoexyz.com.

FYI: Trader Joe is a decentralized exchange based on the Avalanche blockchain.

4. Switch to the *Trade* menu item, exchange the desired amount of AVAX for TIME and confirm the transaction. Transaction costs will apply.

6. Visit the homepage https://app.wonderland.money and connect your wallet.

7. Switch to the *Stake* menu item.

8. Select the desired amount of TIME tokens, confirm the transaction via the STAKE button and via your *wallet*. Transaction costs will apply.

9. You will then receive rewards in the form of the MEMO token. These can subsequently be exchanged 1:1 for TIME.

RELATED LINKS

I have used affiliate links to fund this book. This means I receive small commissions when you purchase products from my partners. This has no influence on the price you pay. Sometimes, you even get paid a bonus yourself. The commissions are usually very similar for all providers. As a result, I can also find the best products for you unselfishly and conscientiously. Please use this opportunity to support me:

Ledger Nano:
https://shop.ledger.com?r=34684ea950dc

Cake DeFi: https://cakedefi.com/?ref=074201

Binance:
https://www.binance.com/de/register?ref=SXIL0YZL

Nexo: https://t1p.de/1iymj

Furthermore, I recommend you visit my online blog about FinTech, investment and cryptocurrencies:
https://www.lazy-investing.com/

GLOSSARY

A

automated market maker (AMM): a method to build prices according supply and
demand on decentralized exchanges

C

CeDeFi: *Centralized Decentralized Finance*
CeFi: Centralized Finance / traditional financial system ·
collateralization ratio: ratio of a collateral to the loan amount

---

D

dApps: Decentralized Applications
DeFi: Decentralized Finance
DEX: Decentralized Exchange

F

fiat money: centralized money that is issued by governmental institutions, e.g. Euro,
Dollar etc.
full nodes: A computer with the full data of the blockchain, usually also a validator for
blockchain transactions

K

KYC: Know Your Customer

L

liquidity pool: a collection of funds locked in a smart contract

loan-to-value (LTV): metric to evaluate the risk of a loan

LP: Liquidity Provider

P

Proof of Stake (PoS): Consensus method that uses the amount of deposited coins (stake) for the validation process in a blockchain

proof of work (PoW): Consensus method that uses computing power to validate transactions

private key: password for a crypto wallet

public key: public account number of a wallet

T

total value locked (TVL): key metric that shows how much capital (in US-Dollar) is deposited in DeFi Applications

---

V

validation: refers to the validation process of transactions in a blockchain

---

W

wallet: an account to save cryptocurrencies and transfer them via blockchain

Wallet: entspricht einem persönlichen Konto, auf dem Kryptowährungen gespeichert

Sources:

Pictures: Canva.com

https://app.defisaver.com/

https://blockchainwelt.de/dapp-dezentralisierte-app-dapps/

https://blockchainwelt.de/token-coin-unterschied/

https://blog.chainalysis.com/reports/2021-crypto-crime-report-intro-ransomware-scams-darknet-markets

https://coinarbitragebot.com/de/arbitrage.php

https://coinarbitragebot.com/de/market.php?

https://coinmarketcap.com/

https://coinmarketcap.com/de/currencies/ethereum/

https://cryptorank.io/price/defichain/arbitrage

https://defichain.com/learn/swap-and-arbitrage/

https://defichain.com/white-paper/

https://defiprime.com/risks-in-defi

https://defirate.com/lend/?exchange_table_type=lend

https://docs.soliditylang.org/en/v0.8.6/introduction-to-smart-contracts.html,

https://doi.org/10.1093/jfr/fjaa010

https://ethdocs.org/en/latest/contracts-and-transactions/account-types-gas-and-transactions.html

https://ethereum.org/de/what-is-ethereum/

https://finematics.com/history-of-defi-explained/

https://finematics.com/impermanent-loss-explained/

https://winheller.com/blog/decentralized-finance-defi-lending-steuern/,

https://www.bpb.de/politik/wirtschaft/finanzmaerkte/51718/banken

https://www.cryptostudio.com/de/lending/aave/

https://www.cryptostudio.com/de/lending/nexo/

https://www.erights.org/smart-contracts/

https://www.forbes.com/sites/ilkerkoksal/2019/09/29/the-shift-toward-decentralized-finance-why-are-financial-firms-turning-to-crypto/

https://www.foxbusiness.com/features/mighty-ducks-actor-brock-pierce-used-Bitcoin-to-buy-1-2m-home-in-amsterdam

https://www.reddit.com/r/defi/comments/r6qvqq/the_reason_people_think_defi_is_so_complicated_is/

https://www.stakingrewards.com/earn/wrapped-Bitcoin/overview/

https://www.stakingrewards.com/providers/
https://www.tokens24.com/de/cryptopedia/basics/ist-usdt-und-wie-funktioniert-es

https://www.winheller.com/bankrecht-finanzrecht/Bitcointrading/Bitcoinundsteuer/besteuerung-liquidity-mining-defi.html

https://www.youtube.com/c/julianhosp

DISCLAIMER
Disclaimer for contents of this e-book

The contents of this e-book have been created with the utmost care. However, I can not guarantee the accuracy, completeness and timeliness of the content. The owner of this e-book page assumes no liability for any damage caused by the use of the information provided here. The use of information from this e-book or on websites accessible by link is exclusively at the risk of the user. By using this e-book the user agrees to the terms and conditions stated herein. The owner of this book may change the terms of use at any time. If this e-book continues to be used after the terms of use have been changed, the changed terms are considered accepted.

The provided offer does not constitute a securities trading service, financial or investment advice. The offer provided by the operator here is only intended to provide information to the consumer. Should the consumer purchase securities or financial services of any kind on the basis of the information provided here, he does so on his own decision and consideration and acts at his own risk and responsibility.

The operator nor its employees, collaborators or authors can provide any guarantee or warranty for the performance, price and development trends of securities, shares, derivatives, real estate, commodities, precious metals, bonds, currencies, cryptocurrencies and other mentioned financial and investment products and/or financial services expressed or forecast in the information provided. The consumer is aware that factors or circumstances can occur at any time, which make predicted or expressed performance, price and development trends invalid. It is expressly pointed out that the business with cryptocurrencies is not suitable for everyone. There is basically the risk of losses, up to the total loss of the invested capital.

Copyright

Imprint

Eduard Meider, Berlin

Contact: info@lazy-investing.com

Dispute resolution

We are not willing or obligated to participate in dispute resolution proceedings before a consumer arbitration board.

Liability for contents

As a service provider, we are responsible for our own content on these pages in accordance with the general laws pursuant to § 7 para. 1 TMG. According to §§ 8 to 10 TMG, however, we are not obligated as a service provider to monitor transmitted or stored third-party information or to investigate circumstances that indicate illegal activity.

Obligations to remove or block the use of information under the general laws remain unaffected. However, liability in this regard is only possible from the point in time at which a concrete infringement of the law becomes known. If we become aware of any such infringements, we will remove the relevant content immediately.

Liability for links

Our offer contains links to external websites of third parties, on whose contents we have no influence. Therefore, we cannot assume any liability for these external contents. For the contents of the linked pages is responsible for the content of the linked pages. The linked pages were checked for possible legal violations at the time of linking. Illegal contents were not recognizable at the time of linking. However, a permanent control of the contents of the linked pages is not reasonable without concrete evidence of a violation of the law. If we become aware of any infringements, we will remove such links immediately.

Copyright

Privacy policy

The links marked with *, are affiliate links. This ebook is funded by affiliate links. This means that if you purchase a product from my partners, the owner of the ebook will receive a commission. This does not affect the price you pay. Since the commissions are usually very similar for all providers, I can also find the best products for you unselfishly and to the best of my conscience.

To be able to track the origin, the operator of the products stores cookies in your browser. This is how the company recognizes that you have clicked on an affiliate link via the ebook.

Cookies

Our website uses HTTP cookies to store user-specific data. Below, we explain what cookies are and why they are used so that you can better understand the following privacy policy.

What exactly are cookies? Whenever you browse the Internet, you use a browser. Popular browsers include Chrome, Safari, Firefox, Internet Explorer, and Microsoft Edge. Most websites store small text files in your browser. These files are called cookies.

One thing can't be denied: Cookies are really useful little helpers. Almost all websites use cookies. More precisely, they are HTTP cookies, as there are other cookies for other applications. HTTP cookies are small files that are stored on your computer by our website. These cookie files are automatically placed in the cookie folder, effectively the "brain" of your browser. A cookie consists of a name and a value. When defining a cookie, one or more attributes must also be specified. Cookies store certain user data about you, such as language or personal page settings. When you return to our site, your browser transmits the "user-related" information back to our site. Thanks to cookies, our site knows who you are and offers you your usual default setting. In some browsers, each cookie has its own file; in others, such as Firefox, all cookies are stored in a single file.

There are both first-party cookies and third-party cookies. First-party cookies are created directly by our site, third-party cookies are created by partner websites (e.g. Google Analytics). Each cookie must be evaluated individually, as each cookie stores different data. Also, the expiration time of a cookie varies from a few minutes to a few years. Cookies are not software programs and do not contain viruses, Trojans or other "pests". Cookies also cannot access information on your PC.

What types of cookies are there?

The question of which cookies we use in particular depends on the services used and is clarified in the following sections of the privacy policy. At this point, we would like to briefly discuss the different types of HTTP cookies.

We can distinguish between 4 types of cookies:

Absolutely necessary cookies.

These cookies are necessary to ensure basic functions of the website. For example, these cookies are needed when a user adds a product to the shopping cart, then continues browsing on other pages, and only later goes to the checkout. These cookies do not delete the shopping cart even if the user closes his browser window.

Functional cookies

These cookies collect information about user behavior and whether the user receives any error messages. In addition, these cookies are also used to measure the loading time and the behavior of the website with different browsers.

Target-oriented cookies

These cookies provide a better user experience. For example, entered locations, font sizes or form data are stored.

Advertising cookies

These cookies are also called targeting cookies. They are used to deliver customized advertising to the user. This can be very convenient, but also very annoying.

Usually, when you visit a website for the first time, you are asked which of these cookie types you want to allow. And of course, this decision is also stored in a cookie.

How can I delete cookies?

How and whether you want to use cookies is up to you. Regardless of which service or website the cookies come from, you always have the option to delete, only partially allow or disable cookies. For example, you can block third-party cookies, but allow all other cookies.

If you want to find out which cookies have been stored in your browser, if you want to change or delete cookie settings, you can find it in your browser settings:

Chrome: Delete, enable and manage cookies in Chrome.

Safari: Manage cookies and website data with Safari.

Firefox: Delete cookies to remove data that websites have placed on your computer.

Internet Explorer: delete and manage cookies

Microsoft Edge: delete and manage cookies

If you generally don't want cookies, you can set your browser to notify you whenever a cookie is about to be set. This way, you can decide for each individual cookie whether or not to allow it. The procedure varies depending on the browser. The best way is to search for the instructions in Google with the search term "delete cookies Chrome" or "disable cookies Chrome" in case of a Chrome browser or replace the word "Chrome" with the name of your browser, e.g. Edge, Firefox, Safari.

Made in the USA
Las Vegas, NV
14 September 2022

55317908R00075